# OUR LIVES
# OUR VOICES
# OUR MUSIC

# OUR LIVES
# OUR VOICES
# OUR MUSIC

CHARLES DAVID BROOKS, III

**Publisher's Note**

ISBN-13: 978-1495202025
ISBN-10: 149520202X

Library of Congress Control Number: 2014904268
Brooks, Charles, III, 1939-

Federal Writers' Project historical documents are used by permission of the Library of Congress.

**Cover art** rendered by Sandy Williams (Pratt Institute, New York, 1963), as an art assignment to paint Charles David Brooks, III as he would look 30 years later.

For information on the content of this publication, please contact Mr. Charles David Brooks, III at charlesbrooks9686@att.net or call 803-661-3961.

**Published by WrightStufco**
**Printed in the United States of America**

To the spiritual essence of the instance of the creation of my eternal and internal bloodline; to my parents Charles D. Brooks, Jr. and Ruth C. Brooks; to my ancient ancestors of Fula, Mende, Tembe, Kro, Portuguese, Danish, Scottish, British, LaKota, Cree, Crow, Blackfoot, Seminole, Cherokee, and East India; to my audience on 125th Street and 8th Avenue during WWII; to PS54k, Boys High School (Brooklyn), LACC, UCLA, Columbia U; and to Benedict College, do I dedicate this book of plays.

# CONTENTS

OUR LIVES OUR VOICES OUR MUSIC 1

AFFAIRS OF OUR ANCESTORS 13

HELP! 39

SHELTER 79

THE BROTHERS by Publius Terentius Afer
(Terence) 114

# ACKNOWLEDGEMENTS

Many people have supported my efforts while I continued to express myself as I journey through this barren land writing, directing, and producing theatre that promote an awareness as to what surrounds us as a people. Included in that number are the following; Dorothy Richardson, Ruby Watts, Juanita Scott, Gregg Levy, Shirley Elmore, Sean Daniels, Doris Johnson, Gerald Hunt, Corin Diggs, Herman Jones, Jr., Alicia Briggs, Kymm Hunter, Wendell Brown, Trustus Theatre, Yvonne Somerville, Arneshia Williams, Toretha Wright, and the cast and crew of the BC Theatre Ensemble (2000 to 2014).

My sons, Charles, Saeed, David, and Solomon, inspire me greatly; watching them grow and develop into manhood, including my grandsons. I was not that fortunate to see my other sons grow and develop, yet they have always been with me in thought, prayer, and meditation. However, it is in writing that I often wrap dialogue around my characters that is meant for them.

# PREFACE

*I*n accordance with my family's oral traditions as the eldest son, I received privileges of serving my father as he lead discussion meetings among men in his gatherings. Likewise, I served my mother as she lead meetings among the women in her gatherings, as long as I kept my mouth shut and only listened in on the discussions. These discussions recorded deep into my Brain Eye as my perceptions of political, social, economic, and physical environments shaped me as to how I see through the matrix white America tried to present to me. While attending elementary school, some white teachers made attempts to teach me about Greek and Roman empires as being the beginning of civilizations and that all things in culture had evolved from them as through I did not have sense enough to see through their deceptions. At an early age, I read up on Greeks and the Romans: Plato, Socrates, Aristotle, Herodotus, Euripides, Sophocles, Plautus, Terence, and others as their writings lead me to Kemet.

After spending 70 years as a dancer, singer, songwriter, actor, director, poet, playwright, and producer, my knowledge of theater developed through the experiences of other performers who related to me of their experiences in the world of theater around the globe. It is my desire that students of theater and theater history will begin to gain additional insight into the origin of African Theater from the Nile Valley to South Africa, and its evolution throughout the various civilizations. After teaching theater to thousands of students from west and east coast, and more recently, Benedict College I realized the need of knowledge of African Theater. I observed how African American students learning of theater from as far back as 8500 BCE to African dramatists of the Greco Roman Classical period tend to become more motivated in expressing their ideas and themes of life.

They became ready to get in touch with their innermost thoughts without fears of being branded as unique or odd for thinking and dreaming of having a history. More importantly, they began to research and to read plays to discover societal influences shaping themselves. Benedict College students are more concerned about who they are rather than constantly being bombarded by who the dominant society is with its Greco Roman heritage of killings fathers, marrying mothers, homosexual love affairs, betrayal, and the right to kill their mothers, as depicted in their plays.

African theater and African Diaspora theater assist our students in learning how to identify themselves, understanding certain notions of self-awareness, purpose of unity, independence, belief values of elders and most of all, aware of ancestral spirits.

## *Making of a Griot*

As I indicated earlier, my childhood life explored the vessels of my ancestors through oral history whether they be from Africa, Brazil, Cuba, Portuguese (Gee-Gee), Cherokee, Cree, Blackfoot, Crow, or Ireland, Scotland, and British. My Elders taught me all about them, most times by names, period, countries, events, and good or not so good deeds, beliefs, values, customs, traditions, and as to how each got along with the others. They eventually became divided due to political, social and economical lines drawn as to who was black, red or white, and as to who, what, where, when, and how they survived. I witnessed those who decided to pass, or return to the reservations, and those who would remain true to the cause of Africa. Before the division, all members of my family gave input into who I am today ... a Playwright and a Griot.

At an early age, I passed down to my younger sisters and brother what was passed down to me. I am regarded in my family as the one with the oral history. As time went on, my knowledge expanded to include peoples from all over the world, especially of people who had been oppressed. I began to write one man shows with music and dance to reflect my thoughts relevant to current events bridging oral history as a measurement of how far we as a people had come and to where we are today. Benedict College students have been supportive of my works as a playwright and griot. My work consists of narratives set to music, dance and the spoken word.

My works have been known to penetrate a subliminal membrane shielding the Brain's Eye from receiving knowledge while enlightening students as to their purpose as scholars and scientists. My plays' genre range from ritual, to spiritual, to a one man show with instruments to a cast of many; reflecting many thoughts which are not expressed by some due to the code that exists since the capturing and redistribution of African prisoners into slavery.

Our Lives Our Voices Our Music reveals ancient ancestral characters emerging from the spiritual world to enlighten humankind of its misdeeds to humanity. From the earliest of time, our ancestral past revealed a plan for resurrection and redemption. It was as though our ancestors predestined that plan for us today to lift the veil and to open the third (or cosmic) eye for enlightenment. Any one of these ancestral characters can be you, or waiting to come from within you. See and listen for the keys to the ancestral realm; you can unlock the mystery box that opens up into a new creation. However, you must be willing to change. The question becomes, "Change from what to what?" To change, you must find who the man or woman in the mirror really is. Get in touch with your Power of Imagination ... "you will see the light...the light will set you free ... For in the beginning was darkness ... then there was light..."

# OUR LIVES OUR VOICES OUR MUSIC

## A One Act Play

### CHARACTERS

NARRATOR
TEHUTI
MA'AT
ISIS
OSIRIS
HORUS
QUEEN MERNEITH
NEPHTHY
PTAH

**TIME:** Between Here and the Here After

**SCENE:** House Curtain is closed. Backstage reveals a scrim with vignettes of our experiences along The Niger River, The Harlem River, The Mississippi River, and the Edisto River which is depicted upon the cyclorama upstage from portal arches, including various effects. Gobos effects are used to create scenes that establish attitude, moods, and scene periods. Up stage center is a circular bandstand covering a saxophone ensemble (conga drum, bells, chimes and a wind instrument may accompany the ensemble). On stage right and stage left are three leveled tiers where chorus of men and women stand. Spaces between stage right and stage left tiers are entrances and exits for dancers. Down stage right is a podium for the narrator. Center stage, in an oval, circular setting, actors are standing and/or lying pressed to the floor with cloths of various traditional designs covering their bodies. Creation is formed by smoke, instruments and dancers as the curtain opens. A man and a woman dressed in white, linen gowns slowing emerge as through, witnessing the forming of creation, looking into space as if looking into heaven, walk toward center

1

stage. Chorus rises from elevator, dressed in robes, stage cross to tiers singing "Blessed Assurance" as instruments fades in and dancers perform a traditional praise dance. Once the chorus, dancers, instruments and light fades, a spot light beams upon stage right revealing an oral traditionalist.

## THE PLAY

NARRATOR: (*In several eastern and Latin languages*) Heus, Bon Matin, Buenos Dias, Dehna Aderu, Karibuni, Maakye, As-salam 'alaykum, Good Morning and/or Good Day. We are all here making History. We have made history from the time we got up this morning. You who have arrived here ... coming from various backgrounds made a decision to make history ... to set a course and pattern for others ... Give yourselves applause. Theatre History tells us through archaeological findings that when you leave Weset (called Thebes by the Greeks) to go down the Nile, passing Dendera where Hathor reigned, you, the traveler, soon comes to al-Balyana, from where you can go overland to Arabat-el-Madfouneth, the barren hamlet which guards the entrance to the antique site of Abdjou (Greek transcribed as Abydos) at the edge of the desert, you will discover the ruins of the Holy City, of Adydos. This region was called Het Ka Ptah. The Greeks transcribed it as Egypt. We shall refer to it as Het Ka Ptah, the land or house of the Spirit. This pilgrimage to Abdjou, during 8500 BCE to 640 AD, drew crowds of pilgrims from all over the Kingdoms to converge on an area around the temple together to celebrate the divine mysteries set to plays as is written in what is now known as the Pyramid Text. The Abdjou Passion Play of Weset depicted resurrection and redemption that has endured to this very day. It was as through these deities of men and women set the course for us to be resurrected and redeemed ... Listen...

TEHUTI: *(To the world)* Life is a series of dilemmas and calamities that will test you and others who become lost...lost and consumed by fire ... flames of pride, greed, lust anger, fear, envy and vanity ... enemies of the Will. Almighty God asks us to give back what He gives to us ... His Own Power ... which is His Will.

MAAT: *(To the world)* My beloved husband ... We must carry forth throughout time ... the plan of redemption and resurrection to enable our people ... who become lost. . .in the wilderness ... the key of repentance ... to unlock the dungeon doors of darkness ... to come into the marvelous light ... to become light to those in shadows of darkness.

TEHUTI: My love ... Let us sit on the Throne of Faith, Wisdom and Truth ... to witness from beyond time the unfolding of darkness from people captured by wanton, carousing, and excessive lust. *(In synchronized movement, Tehuti and Maat stage cross up stage and on thrones prepared for them. Dancers enter as through chained to each other and moving to a Samba and/or Marenge rhythm with loud moans of torture. Instruments wail and chime to the moans of suffering people. Chorus sings "Sometimes I Feel like a Motherless Child" ... as all fades, narrator enters).*

NARRATOR: What you are about to witness is the plight of individuals as they make history freeing themselves from conditioned response of self-imposed shackles of darkness while leaning toward knowledge ... toward light *(instrument ensemble raffs as light intensity reveals a body moving as if rising from beneath a cloth, as narrator exits stage right).*

ISIS: (As if coming out from under a deep sleep being lost in a world that used her to weaken her sons as chorus and sax mums "Amazing Grace" then fades as Isis utters) Aaaaaaaaheeeeeee, humrnmrnrnrn, mmmmrnmm ... what have I allowed myself to do? I have been made to weaken my sons to have strong bodies and weak brains ... not to think things through ... not to make decisions for themselves, their families, and their communities ... their people. I have allowed the enemy without knowing to imprison my sons to become evil carriers of disease, greed, lust, anger and fear. I have been like a chicken ... penned up in a chicken coop...I know I am not a chicken ... somebody help me ... Almighty God... I repent... turn from this world's wicked ways... I turn to your Power, your Will ... (*Isis is in a prayer position as spotlight illumines on the Narrator as other light fades as dancers appear, in silhouette, as if growing from chickens to eagles*).

NARRATOR: Chickens ... There is an African folklore about chickens ... See if you can relate to this... it seems that a British Sea Captain sailed and landed off the coast of Africa. This sea captain marveled at his discovery of such a rich vast land with lots of exotic animals. As he explored the land, he discovered lots of eggs. He gathered up the eggs and sailed with them to a New World. In the New World, he stored the eggs in a huge chicken coop to hatch the eggs and breed them as chickens. As each egg hatched, the sea captain would go... "peep... peep" and the newly hatched egg would go ... "peep ... peep ..." The captain would say "You chicken ... me captain." As each egg hatched, a chicken would say "you chicken ...he captain." Soon, the chicken coop brimmed with chickens ... picking and pecking at each other ... every now and then the captain would give them some water and throw some seeds into the coop. The captain enjoyed watching the chickens run toward the seeds picking and pecking. One day, the Captain found a wounded eagle near death. The captain put the eagle in the chicken coop. The eagle looked bad ... all beaten up ... weaken by the loss of blood. The chickens gathered near the eagle and complained that the eagle should not be there ... with them ...because the eagle was not like them ... chickens ... they laughed, making jokes about how ugly the eagle looked. They were glad they were not like him. As time grew on, the eagle began to gain strength. One day the eagle tested the strength of his wings. He stretched them out wide, flapping them up and down (*dancers mimicking the narration*). The chicken gathered together in fear ... "what kind of creature is this"? The eagle lifted up in flight landing on top of the coop, spreading his wings out wide, casting a shadow down upon the others. The eagle looked at them and saw that they were eagles that their wings had been clipped. He said, "You are eagles like me ... spread your wings ... "They replied, "No ... we are not eagles ... we are chickens ... "The eagles felt compassion for his brothers and sisters because they did not know they too were eagles. The eagle lifted up and began to soar high into the sky. He circled the chicken coop swooping down and flying high. "Join me ... join me," he said. They replied, "No ... we are chickens." In the far corner of the chicken coop, two chickens made discoveries as they began to spread their wings and running to lift off but falling each time. The eagle saw this and flew to them immediately. The eagle worked with the two newly discovered eagles and taught them to fly. The eagle lifted off with the two eagles lifting off behind him. They were so very happy to be able to fly as they shouted out, "We are eagles ...look everybody we can fly ... we all are eagles ... come join us and let us flyaway." (*Dancers as eagles beckon audience members to fly*) But it was sad to see eagles maintaining a claim to be chickens because they were taught and conditioned to be chickens that they believed they were chickens. The huge eagle made one more pass over the chicken coop, with the two eagles at his wing tips, and said, "It is not time yet for them to realize who and what they are, perhaps we will come back for them later and then hopefully they will be ready to join us. As the eagles soared to the highest heights of the heavens ... those in the chicken coop hovered together crying that they were chickens ... only some had some thoughts that perhaps they too could fly (*Narrator's Light fades as Light illuminates upon Isis*).

ISIS: (*Isis is strengthen by Light as the chorus and Sax ... very lightly sings "I Believe I Can Fly ... dancers appears as if growing from chickens to eagles, spreading their wings in movement as all begin to rise in movement).* I am no longer a chicken caught up in a chicken coop... I am an Eagle (*as she flexes her wings*). I believe I can fly... I believe I can fly... I believe I can fly. I can fly! Thank you Lord (*as chorus mums "I Believe I Can Fly"... chorus, instruments and dancers interact with each other ... an eagle appears to support Isis joined by dancers as they fly up stage left and right and... singing "I Believe I Can Fly"...Isis to the throne).*

OSIRIS: (*Dancers return in Vanity, pride, self-conceit and delusion reflecting Osiris movements as intensity of light illuminates around him ... as he rises pantomiming a mirror in his hand*) Look! Hold up my mirror for the world to see that beauty is not in the eyes of the beholder but beauty is within me. When earthly angels sing they call out my name ... not because of my fortune or fame ... but because to them, my people. I am their Nubian King. I am the color of the darkest soil ... hair the texture of lamb's wool. My eyes tell the story of ancient kings and queens ... my voice is the echo of our ancestors' scream. The marks that adorn my body are all the dreams that have been split down the seams. The tears that flow represent all of those innocent children who lost their lives in pursuit of the American Dream. My veins flow the blood that kept an African king; my brain is the only weapon that is capable of driving men and women insane. I have been separated from the members of my body, yet my blood flow through all members wherever they may be scattered ... I am the Great Diaspora... I am dead, yet I live, look into the mirror and you can see me ... Remember me ... as you search yourselves ... You will be everywhere, yet like the river you must return to the sea...I am the River .. .I am the River Niger ... Hear my waters (*Chorus sings "Kum Ba Yah, My Lord" ... Conga drum, chimes, woodwind, and sax plays, Osiris and dancers stage cross to throne. Narrator steps out*).

NARRATOR: Through the Great Diaspora, master builders,

artisans, priests, kings and queens, prophets and prophetess were scattered throughout the new world into the Western Hemisphere, in south and north Americas and in the Caribbean ... These children of Almighty God learned the languages of their captors ... But just like the River they will eventually return to the open sea ... Like salmon they will consistently fight upstream to breed a new nation ... a new civilization ... a new beginning ... willing to die ... to live     (*Narrator exits*).

HORUS: (*The Black National Anthem is heard very low throughout as Horus rises*) Just like the River, David Walker's Appeal is a tool for revolution. He aroused slaves of the South into rebelling against their master. His tool is a document described as "for a brief and terrifying moment the most notorious document in America" David Walker was born in Wilmington, North Carolina, perhaps in 1796 or 1797. Since his mother was a free black, David Walker was also free. He witnessed while in his youth a disturbing episode of a son who was forced to whip his mother until she died. I hope we have not been conditioned to whip our mothers until they die. Huh! You wouldn't whip your mother ... would you? Men and women like Walker fared well setting up their own business like Walker's Used Clothing Store during the 1820. We don't have to kill each other ... We can help each other ... reach out to our brothers and sisters in South America, the Caribbean, even from coast to coast. In September of 1829 David Walker's Appeal reached enslaved men and women of the South while relying on sailors and ship's officers who could transfer his pamphlet to southern ports. This brother was awesome; Walker even used his clothing business which was located close to the waterfront to serve sailors. He sewed copies of his pamphlet into the lining of sailors' clothing. As these pamphlets reached the South they were distributed throughout the region. We can use our lives ... our voices ... our music ... to unite us. To the slaves the words were inspiring and instilled a sense of pride and hope. There will be danger in uniting. Horrified whites initiated laws that forbade blacks to learn to read and banned the distribution of antislavery literature. Is reading a problem for you? They offered a $3,000 reward for Walker's head, and $10,000 to anyone who could bring him to the South alive ... to kill him. Friends concerned about his safety pleaded with him to flee to Canada. Walker refused by saying, "Somebody must die in this cause, I may be doomed to the stake and the fire, or the scaffold tree, but it is not in me to falter if I can promote the work of emancipation." I no longer have a desire to take drugs or alcohol... tools of progressive death? I rather die changing the man in the mirror than dying for a cheap high. Walker, a devout Christian, believed that his work was a "glorious and heavenly cause!' Yet, they tried to scandalize his name. Are we as a people doing anything about our own lives? Are we willing to stand up as men and women? Or would we rather die with our backs to the wall? (*Horus stares into the audience, Queen Merneith rises, instruments playing*).

QUEEN MERNEITH: (*Taking a deep breath ... seeing for the first time ... in a while*) Horus ... Horus...I need to tell you something. Let us not forget how we got here! Booker T. Washington said to "To those of my race who depend on bettering their condition in a foreign land, or who underestimate the importance of cultivating friendly relations with the Southern white man, who is their next door neighbor, I would say: "Cast down your bucket where you are" cast it down in making friends, in every manly way, for the people of all races by whom we are surrounded. We need to unite! It was Booker T. who, in 1916, invited Marcus Garvey of Jamaica, West Indies to visit him at Tuskegee. Garvey was about liberation from the psychological bondage of racial inferiority. Garvey envisioned a great shipping line to foster black trade, to transport passengers between America, the Caribbean, and Africa, and to serve as a symbol of black grandeur and enterprise. Don't you want to meet your blood relatives living within these Americas to bond? Yes ... like Horus said...it is dangerous. Because the fear of a "redeemer" ... a "Black Moses", Garvey was sentenced to prison. Garvey was deported back to Jamaica in November 1927. He never returned to America. Who among you are willing to pick up the Liberation flag and stand up for Justice? "By the God of Heaven, we are cowards and jackasses if now that the war is over, we do not marshal every ounce of our brain and brawn to fight the forces of hell in our own land," cried W.E.B. DuBois to my people in his day. As a woman I have been scandalized...I have been called everything but a child of God ...Sometimes I felt like a motherless child ... Do you know what I mean? Have you felt that way ... Horus? Oh, Precious Lord, hear my pains ... turn my anger from destructive things to self and others to your will that I can become a Mother to my children. That I can become a Mother to a new civilization; a civilization that will overcome those who have rebelled against me and against your Will ... hear me Almighty God ... hear my words ... listen to my heart, see my soul ... see my spirit ... shed your beam of light upon me that my little light may shine so other can see. Give life to my people ... who have been weaken with dry bones ... Release us from the Lust of the flesh, from alcohol, drugs and wanton sex. (*Spotlight beams upon them, chorus sings "Precious Lord" ... Praise dancers offers their hand to Horus and Queen Merneith and leads him to the throne as Narrator enters*).

NARRATOR: Martin Luther King, Junior had a Dream and he was killed ... Malcolm X embraced Islam and he were killed ... Paul Robeson spoke out against oppression and he was rejected and blackballed. We have seen individuals overcome personal calamities and dilemmas in their lives. We have witnessed powerful revelations. Now let listen to Nephthy, an attorney, who will cause you to make a decision concerning justice and fair play ... our ancestors called for justice and fair play, our parents have called for justice and fair play ... we are calling for justice and fair play from Caesar ... mmmmm ... the Supreme Court of the Land. (*Narrator draws attention to Nephthy*) Rise ...

Rise up Nephthy!

NEPHTHY: (*Nephthy rises… looks into the eyes of the audience as Jurors … she stage cross right and left … she stage cross downstage center… looking at a lone juror in the rear of the house.*) Will you give me your fullest attention … ? Will you allow your brain to let my voice come into your thoughts…? Will you do that now…? Now close your eyes and listen … and imagine on what I have to say to you. Think for a moment; try to remember where you were on September 11, 2001...the day known as 9-1-1. 9-1-1 is known all over the land as an emergency code for help. Think through this with me … were you surprised? Do you think some people thought this was an act of God? That this was not our problem? That what goes around comes around? That you knew something was going to happen? Now imagine being laid out like sardines in a can … only this is the bottom level of a ship … called the Middle Passage where many of our ancestors were chained together by neck, ankles and waist. Between the 18th and 19th centuries, African or rather Black people were captured as prisoners, tortured, maimed and made to lie in a ship like sardines in a can. Our ancestors were chained, lying in stench from urine and feces. Many people died from terror brought on by the unknown … many people threw themselves over board when they got the chance … and followed their dead as food for the fish … rather than to continue into the abyss of terror and fear. Yet, those people who endured terror of the unknown, of the mystery that was set before them … when they moaned … were their moans a call for 9-1-l? And think about those brothers and sisters, in places like Mississippi, South Carolina, and elsewhere in this foreign land, hung for remembering their native lands, their languages and their cultures, while demanding human rights … while the others watched in terror … were they calling 9-1-1? When Emmitt Till was wrapped in barbed wire and dragged through the Mississippi River mud, then tied to a tree, and near death, made to watch being castrated... seeing alcohol poured on his testicles and set afire while his captors danced howling around him ... in Emmitt's tortured dying moments ... was he calling for 9-1-l? Four little girls attending Sunday church services, in Alabama, filled with praising Almighty God ... lives were wrecked and shattered by a bomb ... packed with hate... Did they died calling 9-1-1? Myrlie Evers and Coretta Scott King, did they call 9-1-1 when their husbands were murdered, in cold blood, by hate and envy because of Dr. Martin Luther King, Jr. and Medgar Evers struggle for human rights for their people? Shock, horror and terror lifted off of the printed news when in Jasper, Texas a brother was dragged along a country road from behind a pick-up truck driven by hate ... Why are you here? You must make a decision... if we as a people ... throughout these Americas ... north and south ... are going to survive ... then we must overcome Racism ... we must challenge and be challenged on a course called "Change." We must change the way we think ... change ... the way we walk ... change the way we talk ... we must unite in Spirit and change the way we live ... then We Shall Overcome! (*Chorus and instruments sing We Shall Overcome*)... STAND UP ... ON YOUR FEET ... HOLD ARMS THE WAY WE USE TO LINK OURSELVES TO EACH OTHER ... NOW SING. (*Actors and dancers link arms as all voices rise to the song as the song is ending Ptah rises and begin waving his arms for all to stop and sit down all stop and stare at him*).

PTAH: I don't know about all of you but I am going to make me some money. It's about making that green ... right! With money, I can buy respect... Everybody will know me ... (*dancers and actors leave upstage left and upstage right*) ... Money can buy me love ... if I want it too ... (*a dancer, in mask, enters holding a mirror up before Ptah who does not recognize the man in the mirror ... the Master Builder*) Who is that? Hey that's not me in the mirror? He looks like someone I've seen in a book on Ancient History ... When I was in college ... Why don't I see my face? What is this telling me? Am I looking from inside out...Is that me? Was that me? He seems to know what I am thinking ... But I can't tell what he is thinking... I need to get myself together ... too much drugs and alcohol I can't think right... (*Ptah sits down ...dancer with mirror leaves*). Who am I? I need to change my mind... (*Underneath Ptah thoughts chorus begins to sing "Soon Ah Will Be Done*). Where is everybody? (*A cell cast upon the stage by light effects*)... Wait a minute... I am in prison. (*Actors enter in circular position around Ptah*)... How did I get here? I didn't do nothing ... Hey somebody let me out of here ... (*Dancers enter in a ritual dance*).

ACTORS: Ptah come out of that flesh ... Be yourself ... Do ... Be yourself ... Be who you are...

PTAH: Who is Ptah? Am I Ptah? Am I the Master Builder? (Ptah falls on his knees and as he quivers with shakes) Ahhhhhhhhhhhhhhhhhhhaaaaaaaaaaaaa
Whatever is in me ... come forth.

ACTORS AND DANCERS: Ptah...Ptah... Ptah...
PTAH: (*Ptah rises standing regal as the light effects fades*) I am free at last... Thank God Almighty...I am free at last. (*A medley of song and dance takes place as everyone is on stage, curtain slowing close as Narrator steps forward*) and say...

NARRATOR: The end is your beginning.

# AFFAIRS OF OUR ANCESTORS

Affairs of Our Ancestors depicts an ancient spiritual council assembling in order to relate to this present generation the need to rise up and stand up, stay up, and to bring awareness to this world. These ancient ancestors moved me spiritually to write about them so that their open-mouth could speak to the youth, young adults, and older adults. During the writing of Affairs, I could feel their spirits rising within me as they dictated to me as to what is to be. It was as if the ancestral spirits wanted to look out, though me, into the modern world from the realm of the afterlife. Affairs came to me as a vision from our ancestral spirits.

## THE PLAY

## ACT I

## CHARACTERS
The Ancestral Spirits

| | |
|---|---|
| AKHENATON | The Creator of Monotheism |
| IMHOTEP | The World First Known Genius |
| NEFERTITI | Queen of Kemet |
| NZINGA | Amazon Queen |
| MAKEDA | Queen of Sheba |
| CANDACE | Empress of Ethiopia |
| HANNIBAL | Ruler of Carthage |
| DAHIA AL KAHINA | Queen Kahina |
| BEHANZIN HOSSU BOWELLE | The King |

**TIME:** Eternal

**LOCATION:** The After-life: It is somewhere between 12500 BCE and the present.

**MUSIC:** A continuous sound of ancient African music heard barely in the background as musical sounds leak in and out, flute, violin, African drums, rattles, voices, etc. Ancient incense is burning slightly. There are pillars with globes on top of them emitting light from them. There is a pyramid in the background with a sphinx nearby. The cyclorama reveals a clear blue sky with white clouds with distance effects. We see a mist of clouds flowing across the stage, a spinning light flash all around the house and the playing stage. Stage light revealed along the stage lip from left to right as lighting become dimmer toward upstage area where strip lighting leaks down along the cyclorama down onto the upstage flooring. There are thirteen empty thrones situated upstage in a circular shape awaiting the seating of a spiritual council. As the clouds subside, dancers dressed in ancient cloths, headdress, small bells around their ankles, dance an ancient mystical dance, __ an ancient old man shouts to the Heavens ... SHANGO...SHANGO SHANGO...Lightning and Thunder Are Heard In the Background... Dancers dance frenzy as they summon the Ancient Ancestral Spirits ... a single light finds Akhenaton center stage.

**SCENE:** Somewhere in the after-life, Akhenaton, the first ruler in recorded history to believe in the concept of One God, is sitting center stage, dressed in white, wearing a high crown, carrying an ankh in his left hand and a staff in his right hand, in a trance like state of thought, meditating on the One God. Akhenaton rises. He crosses downstage, the ankh leading in his left hand, the staff in his right hand. Akhenaton stage cross along the lip of the stage looking into the world of cultures. He sees remnants of his influence into today's society. Akhenaton sighs in pain and grief as he stares fixed into the world. Akhenaton take a half turn toward stage left and if in a semi-circle he stage cross to his throne and sits upright with his eyes focused upward toward the sun. He speaks.

AKHENATON: Almighty God, You revealed your presence to me thousands of years ago as a veil in my weakest moment when I was all alone (*He pauses*). I am graceful with gratitude for your presence. I revealed your name to the world as your people knelt in reverence exclaiming Amen thousands of years ago. Now as I sit here all alone again from the after-life, I call upon your presence as I honor, praise, and glorify your Spiritual Power to intervene into the life of mankind all over the sea of cultures to spare them from thou mighty wrath to come (*He pauses*). What happened to them Almighty God? How did the people get so far away from Thee? Oh Creative Essence men and women have no respect for each other. They have orgies and call sex love as they prance with the Satyr. Children are to fend for themselves as they are sacrifice giving up their lives to sexual disease, lies, deception and war. There is misery all around. Wars are fought under false pretense. There is deception everywhere in the land and national leaders mislead their people. Men and women act like gods and goddesses and have become lovers of each other and of themselves. You asked me to reveal your presence to the world and that there is only One God. Yet as I look toward the West, I see people worshiping idols in the form of chemical drugs and sex and becoming addicted to feelings. Whom can we send into their world this day to turn them from their wicked ways? I pray Thee ... send me a word from a messenger! (*While Akhenaton is kneeling before his throne, Imhotep enters from stage left with a mallet and chisel in his hand. As Akhenaton rises to return to his throne, Imhotep stage cross stage center, dressed in green, wearing a black skullcap. He speaks*)

IMHOTEP: Eat, drink, and be merry for tomorrow we shall die. What is the measure of a man? Is it his knowledge? What is his knowledge? Is it his character? (*Akhenaton stage crosses down center to Imhotep*) As an architect, astronomer, philosopher, poet and physician, I have studied the attachment of man and of woman and their loneliness in this world. This world filled with confusion and chaos. I have found that each person possesses various lives depending upon the circumstance and the situation. Therefore, they are never their true selves.

AKHENATON: Imhotep, I looked for you in this after-life. How is it that you appear to me now!

IMHOTEP: It is only now that your thoughts revealed compassion for humankind as it was you who revealed the One God to the world during your lifetime. You believed that the world would conform to a divine order. You did not take into account that this world would be of various cultures, beliefs, values and deities. In addition, you did not take into account that men in the western world view themselves as God. As I look out into their worlds of today I see sadness, anger and loneliness in their lives.

AKHENATON: Yes! I have observed a new model of human nature in relation to a self-creation of a god emerging, A New World Order. (*Nefertiti enters from stage right. She is dressed in white carrying an ankh and a staff, looking directly into Imhotep's eyes as they place their right hands pressing their straight fingers to their hearts bending their heads in a slight bow. Imhotep stage cross upstage toward the pyramid and sphinx facing them. Nefertiti stands facing Akhenaton*)

NEFERTITI: You are my Pharaoh and my husband.

AKHENATON: Moreover, you are my Queen and wife. (*Nefertiti and Akhenaton face the world standing side by side*)

NEFERTITI: From the 'spiritual' realm, I observed down through the ages a new model of human nature where this new belief considered man primarily as a material entity, whose happiness is measured by his ability to acquire and maintain a material heaven of wealth and pleasure. In this material heaven women are not principals that predicted or participate in social policy, but are objects to be used by men. Viewed as weaker members of this paradise, women cannot be participants in its building. This belief is completely contrary to the beliefs of the ancients and the principals of Maat. In addition, I as a woman desire more from the materialistic realms of man but to a higher 'spiritual' form of being. You, my Pharaoh and husband understood a 'Spiritual Power' working in our lives which developed from an understanding of a "Creative Essence" as the sole creator of all life and that the creative elements of the universe and its relationship to the earth sustain us 'spiritually'.

AKHENATON: You have shared and participated with me in all religious ceremonies. Through our combined efforts, the 'Creative Essence' bestowed blessings upon us. However, you envisioned an active role for women reshaping civilization continuously to maintain a 'spiritual order'.

NEFERTITI: Yes, yet the priests of these new worlds with their materialist model are powerful as they dominate the higher offices of government. In these arenas, women were and still are incapable of divinity as men dehumanize them with their drugs, money and cars. Together, you and I encountered a revolt by priests, yet we emerged victorious, and created a new capital for Kemet called Akhenaton a city that could give birth to our sacred mission, a mission in pursuit of Divine life. The concept of a woman bypassing the male priest hood to worship the Divine was unacceptable then. And sadly enough, women continue to be unacceptable in the major religions that dominate the world today. Perhaps we can intervene into the lives of our 'children of the light' to redirect their path from darkness and extinction. (*Nefertiti stage cross upstage toward the pyramid and turns observing Akhenaton, while he stage cross toward his throne. Nzinga enters from stage left dressed as a warrior, shouldering a set of arrows and carrying a bow. She is the Amazon Queen of Matamba, West Africa.*)

NZINGA: (Nzinga looks into the audience. She set her bow and arrow as she takes a stance as a warrior and speaks.) I appear before you from the spiritual realm to join this ancestral council that we may intervene into your lives to set you back on track. I am Nzinga I am the one who returned to myself after John of Portugal attempted to assimilate me into someone I was not. I am the one who waged war against the savage slave hunting Europeans for more than thirty years. I am of Angolan descent and I am a symbol of inspiration for people everywhere. At times, some, as Jinga by others as Ginga, know me. I am a member of the ethnic Jagas, a militant group that formed a human shield against the Portuguese slave traders. As a visionary political leader, competent, and self-sacrificing I am completely devoted to the resistant movement. Have you given up the struggle to free yourselves from the worries you find yourselves into? Are you forming allies? I formed alliances with other foreign powers pitting them against one another to free Angola of European influence. Possessed both masculine hardness and feminine charm and I use them both depending upon the situation. I even use religion as a political tool when it suits me. I passed on into the afterlife December 17, 1663. It was only then that the door opened for the massive Portuguese slave trade. Yet my struggle helped awaken others that followed me and forced them to mount offensives against the invaders. These include Madame Tinube of Nigeria: Nandi, the mother of the great Zulu warrior Chaka: Kaipkire of the Herero people of South West Africa: and the female army that followed the Dahomian King, Behanzin Bowelle. You do not struggle for others nor of yourselves ... slaving every day to keep roof over your head, food in your stomach, clothes on your backs are not struggles ... you know how to provide for yourselves ... but you do not do it therefore there is no struggle in you ... SHANGO ... bring forth thyself upon these people ... (*Affonso I enter from stage right. He is wearing a skull crown of gold, dressed in warrior clothing, carrying a staff in his left hand. He approaches Nzinga*).

AFFONSO I: Nzinga

NZINGA: Affonso

AFFONSO I: (*Affonso I bows to salute Nzinga*), Once I submitted to the will of John of Portugal as 1 instructed my people to take on the ways of the Europa as a man of vision who feared a massive onslaught by Europa upon his people. It became my goal to spread my people to the far corners of the earth in various worlds rather than to be cornered by an onslaught and killed in one place. As a visionary, I saw my nation of people, not as a group of separate cultures, but as a unified nation fully equipped with advance knowledge and technology throughout the Universe. (*Affonso I steps to the lip of the stage and spreading his arms towards the whole wide world of today proclaims.*) Nevertheless, I am the first ruler to resist the most despicable act ever known to man; the European slave trade. My nation became divided influenced by Europa and torn apart by wars, famine and disease of all kinds until this very day; especially AIDS, I appear to this 'ancestral spiritual council' to reinforce the need for a 'spiritual intervening' through an intergenerational cultural transmission to our children of the light to get up, stand up, and Be! (*Nzinga bows her head as Affonso I lowers his arms, staring into space as in a trance. He turns towards Nzinga and together they stage cross upstage to their seats. Makeda enters from stage left wearing white apparel, with a white linen hat covering, speaking*).

MAKEDA: Living life to die then to be born into the 'spiritual realm' is a conscious journey never a destination for life goes on in many forms. Ancient black history is suppressed, depressed, oppressed, distorted or ignored by an ungrateful modern world.
Ancient African traditions are so persistent that all of the power and deception of the Western academic establishment have failed to stamp them out. One such story is that of me. I am Makeda, the Queen of Sheba, who journeyed from my land

of Sheba to lands throughout the Persian Empire to union with the Lion of Judah, King Solomon of Israel. King Solomon's character illuminated throughout the known world and I had to journey to meet this Black, wooly head, man and to give birth to our son, Menelik who sat in motion for the seed of the Lions of Judah to come forth. Think about it, you can trace your linkage from Ethiopia Haile Selassie, the Lion of Judah, to King David, back to in the beginning where the River Gihon, known as the Blue Nile River, flows ... read your Bible...I am here from the 'spiritual realm' to remind you ... my sistahs ... Black women of antiquity were and still are legendary for their beauty and power. Especially great were the Queens of Ethiopia who ruled nations of Nubia, Kush, Axum and Sheba. One thousand years before Christ, a line of virgin queens ruled Ethiopia. However, I am the one whose story has survived into your time. My remarkable tradition is recorded in the Kebar Nagast, or the Glory of Kings, and the Bible. Who are you waiting for? You have the Powers my sistahs to rule through a mighty 'Spiritual Being' who has fashioned you to lead. I tell you to tell the other sistahs, not here, to rise up to take their rightful place in society while refusing to allow yourself to be dehumanized by worldly men lusting for the sale of your body. (*Askia Toure, King of Songhai, Candace, Empress of Ethiopia, Hannibal, Ruler of Carthage, Dahia-Al-Kahina, Queen Kahina and Behanzin Hossu Bowelle, the King Shark enters from left and right stage, dressed in their regalia*).

ASKIA: Queen Makeda memories of you will last until the end of time. You represent the mother of long lines of Kings beginning with King Menelik, the seed of King Solomon, who took the real Ark of the Covenant to Ethiopia. Your son, King Menelik, is in a famous line of kings that has continued down to the 20th century when the ruler of Ethiopia the "conquering Lion of Judah" descended directly from you and King Solomon. As for me, I, Askia Tome united the entire central region of the Western Sudan and established a governmental machine that is still revered today for its detail and efficiency. I divided my country into provinces, each with a professional administrator as governor, and ruled each fairly and uniformly through a staff of distinguished legal experts and judges. Yet, as I look out into this western world, from the after-life, I see our 'children of the light' capsuled into a web of legal systems that have entangled their lives to the point that they glorify themselves being locked up and locked down. As I study this situation, I find that they have accepted a mis-educational system as being normal ... and they call it keeping it 'real'. They are being referred to as "Willie's children" as they accept crazy checks, prescribed mind altering drugs that keep them subdued, and a combination of basics as solutions for what it deemed mental deficiencies and learning disabilities deficit in mental, physical, and spiritual growth. I have joined this council to attract an intervening into this world.

CANDACE: Yes, Queen Makeda, your greatness will live forever no one has matched your giving of greatness to the world. Askia, not only Kings have ruled Ethiopia since Menelik, but I, Queen Candace, served as Empress of Ethiopia. I, too, have been discussed in the Bible. As the world's famous military tactician and field commander, I, Candace, broke the world fame and unbroken chain of victories of Alexander-the-Great by halting his armies at the borders of Ethiopia, leading my armies under my personal command. (*Candace stage crosses to the edge of the Lip looks out into the world.*) As I look out into the world, I see the enemy has invaded all of our borders. Through time we witnessed from the 'spiritual realm' destruction of civilizations by wars, slavery, massive killings, death marches, famine, and AIDS, coming from Europa and the west, attacking our people through cities, towns, countryside, and jungles killing millions of people, as the disease spreads throughout the routes of our people as it leaks into the seaports, carried by ships to the Afro-Caribbean, Afro-Latin America and into the seaports of South Carolina seeping into your homes. As we reveal ourselves to you of our greatness in our time we are to remind you of who and whose you are as 'children of the light' you are to rise up so that your children can live.

HANNIBAL: We taught western civilizations how to care for their people through cleanliness, sciences and the arts. Portugal and Spain, because of my leadership did not suffer the Black Plague of the Dark Ages of Europa. Even though, I, Hannibal, as a general and military strategist who ever lived, I used my overpowering African Armies to conquer major portions of Spain, France and Italy defeating the Roman Armies as we marched onward delivering a mighty blow against the Roman Empire. Yet, (*Hannibal stage cross down to the edge of the Lip*) not one of you have raised an army of educators, scientists, and medics to war against and destroy your enemies....AIDS, CANCER, and other diseases, while they kill and destroy millions of people all over the globe, especially among the women and children of African descent Your future is dying right before your eyes. I challenge you to study this situation before it is right up upon you ... AIDS maybe upon you right now and you do not even know it. (*Dahia-Al-Kahina stage crosses down onto the Lip*).

DAHIA-AL-KAHINA: All of you have done exceedingly well in your lifetime and you all have pointed to this world its errors, however it has been Europa's and our cousins who also fought to control us. As Queen Kahiria, I fought against the Arab incursion in North Africa where under my leadership Africans fought back fiercely and drove the Arab army northward into Tripolitana. Wives of African kings committed suicide to avoid falling into the hands of the Berbers and Arabs who showed no mercy to the people who would not be converted to Islam. Now as I look out into the world from the afterlife I see not only weapons of mass destruction destroying my people with chemical, biological, economical, sociological and psychological warfare but also I see SELF-SABOTAGING IN BLACK AMERICA, IN AFRICA, AND BEYOND ... a deeper form of massive suicide ...I appear on this 'ancestral spiritual council' to send a message into this present world that sift you like wheat ... to gain your place on this earth and to meet your ancestral heritage in the after-life with Grace and Dignity ... Let us give way to Behanzin Hossu Bowelle ... (*Behanzin Hossu Bowelle, a strong, bold, might of a man, steps down toward the audience, which is now the world*).

BOWELLE: I have never bowed down to no man ... ever...So...you do not want to know who I am...do you? You see I am that little seed in your brain that they don't want you to know about telling you to do all the things you need to be doing ... that you do not do ... like the fear of losing your woman or your man or your job or your symbols or your gods ... you play with from time to time ... Do you know what I am talking about? When you can stand without wavering... like waves on the oceans ... wavering in and wavering out... If you are afraid to stand for anything then what you have is not worth having ...is it... You see I allow no man ... to see me drink... a glass of water ... because that is personal to me. Men lie ... at my feet ... while I drink water ... and go ... ahhhhhh ... as if they are drinking water ... too. What are you looking at? Are you looking at me or are you reflecting on how personal you have been today and what you could have done and did not do ... Do you know who I am? No, you do not. I am the most powerful ruler in West Africa especially at the end of the 19th century. My army divisions included five thousands female warriors of wonder women. Women of the Gold Coast would rather die than give up their land and their homes to, the invaders ... Yet, I see from the after-life how you throw your women to the dogs in the streets... I see men of today glorifying their bodies with other men. This is a western phenomenon... as you refer to as 'down low brothers' with their 'down low sisters.' Writing, poetry is not new to us...I am a writer of some of the finest song poetry ever written. Yet, as I look into the world you live in today, it is as though I am looking into a box. Can you see what is around you? Can you see your enslavement to technology? I watched you run to your markets buying up all the water you could get for fear of a technology crash from 1999 to 2000. You believed your world would come to an end. You were right ... your world is coming to an end. The Earth will remain as a creation of the Creative Essence ... but your world will end ... Technology is not something new. The Greek playwrights used 'deus ex machina' literally, "the gods from the machine" to control your thoughts. Thoughts are being the fuel that powers the imagination into visualization into actualization. As I look into your box, I see and I hear you using thought as something that never happened. You use your language against yourselves as you speak it ... You do not understand what I am saying ... do you? As I take my seat onto the Council of the Ancestral Spirits a glimpse of your world, through your children, will be reveal and you can see and hear what we see and hear, as we look for a way to intervene into their lives, from the realm of the Spiritual World in the Afterlife. (*Bowelle takes his seat, lightning and thunder and clouds continue as the end of Act I comes to a close*).

## ACT II

## CHARACTERS
The College Students

| | |
|---|---|
| PAUL | President of the Freshman Class |
| SARAH | An Honors Student |
| ROBERT | A Student Athlete |
| MARY | A Junior in Biology |
| JOSEPH | A Senior in Chemistry |
| ELIZABETH | A Freshman in Accounting |

**TIME:** The present

**LOCATION:** College Campus Student Center.

**MUSIC:** New World Order

**SCENE:** Lighting toward center of stage from frontals, left and right side lighting as students are milling around in a lounge area of a student center, reading magazines, listening to music, making out with each other, dressed in regular college life clothing. There is chattering as a loud ringing telephone breaks their noise as they look for the direction in which the telephone is ringing. Some students check their cell phones; the mysterious ringing moves other students. A male student stand and look up toward the ceiling while listening for sound any sound. He reaches for his cell phone and speaks.

PAUL: Hello. (*There is silence.*) Hello ... This is Paul ... Hello...

VOICE: Hello ... Do you hear me now?            .

PAUL: (*Puzzled*) Yes...I hear you now...

VOICE: Is this how I must get your attention? You all are so close to your cell phones ... it is obvious that you do not leave home without them. You carry them everywhere you go, in your classroom, in your churches, in your car, everywhere. I will get your attention. (*All of the students are in shock*).

PAUL: Who are you? Where are you? What do you want from me?

VOICE: I am that I am! I am the Voice of your Ancestral Spirit. I am in the Spiritual World. The Realm of the After-Life!

STUDENTS: What does He want from you Paul?

PAUL: What does He want from me? What does He want from us? The Voice is talking to us. (Sarah stage crosses downstage left toward Paul.)

SARAH: (with fright) Paul, I am afraid. I felt some presence about me all day... today. Something bothers me and this may be the only chance I have to tell you this. (All listen intently)... You see ... I lost my purpose for attending college! I do not know how I let my life come to this. I left home with good intentions ... the first to attend college in my family ... I was going to be the first. .. (*She thinks on what she has said*).

ROBERT: Oh ... Sarah ... you do not have to give up. You can go on with your life ... fulfill your dreams! It is a lot of pressure ...it's nothing wrong with being the first in your family to attend college! Look at me, this college accepted me when no other college would. (*With pride*) Who would have thought it...I am a college student.

MARY: Robert, you forget you are on probation ... and by attending this college is not going to do you any good ... because you only go to class when there is a test ... and your grading are failing grades. You are on probation and maybe suspended the way you are carrying on here. You are living in a world of illusion ... thinking it is real ... the sad part about it is you do not know it yet.

JOSEPH: Nevertheless, Sarah, you are doing well here. You are an Honors student. Your family should be proud of you. What is your problem? You can tell us we are your friends.

SARAH: I think I am pregnant! I maybe ... am ... having a baby!

PAUL: Being pregnant cannot keep you out of college ... can it?

---

MARY: Where is the baby's father? 'Who is the baby's father?

SARAH: He does not want to have anything else to do with me.

MARY: What is the reason he does not want to have anything to do with you?

SARAH: He said he used condoms with me ... and he could not possibly be the father. He does not want to see me any more (everyone is silent). Besides, he now tells me he thinks he has AIDS.

EVERYONE: WHAT! (*They all stare at her*).

SARAH: He says that is how he knows I may not be pregnant.

EVERYONE: HOW?

SARAH: He said that is why he used condoms (*Silence*).

ELIZABETH: Have you gone and been tested yet?

SARAH: No. (*She looks at everyone. They look at her*) I think I am going to sit out this semester.

PAUL: What has come over us? What is this confession time? Huh?

MARY: Old folks say confession is good for the soul.

PAUL: Yeah...Right. I got something to tell you all. (*He holds his head in his hands.*) Someone shot at me the other night.

EVERYONE: WHAT!

PAUL: Yeah, the weapon was pointed toward my head. The bullet almost hit me. I ran for my life. I thought I was going to die ... My life fell down right before my eyes. (*He sobs*).

MARY: Where were you?

PAUL: I was at the club, on Garners Ferry Road.

ROBERT: Garners Ferry Road? What do you know ... about the club ... on Garners Ferry Road ... This is your first semester ... you are not from here ... How did you get there?

PAUL: I went with my dogs...

SARAH: Your dogs almost got you killed...

PAUL: (*With anger*) You should talk about almost killed ... you dead already ... with AIDS!

JOSEPH: That is not nice ... Where did you get money to go to a club?

PAUL: I sold blood ... (*He looks at everyone looking at him*) ... my blood ... two to three pints a week... for the money ... you know to get little things...

ROBERT: To get what little things? You selling your blood. You almost got yourself killed, you reckless man  ... Damn you don't act like you in college ... you act like you on   the   streets somewhere.

ELIZABETH: What are we arguing about? Anything? How do you think our folks back home will think of us? If they knew the truth about us ... about what is going on in our lives.

JOSEPH: I do not know about your folks but my folks believe in me. They think that I may be the One to make a difference in my home and in my community. They think my sisters and brothers will follow in my foot steps and go to college ... because I am the first in my family to attend college. I got to it if not for anyone else... I got to make it for me ... I got too ... (*He holds his head in his hands*).

ELIZABETH: (*She stage crosses to Joseph put her arms around him and says*) Joseph ... Joseph your words are so true to me ... My family back home were all so happy to see me come home during the break. They all expressed how well I am doing in college and how much they are pulling for me to be successful ... and I have not... been able ... (*sigh*) to wake up in the morning ... (*sigh*) to attend my eight o'clock class. I have never attended that class because I felt so ashamed ... when I think how late I would be attending class ... five minutes before it ends. I feel so bad... right now ... like I am letting so many people down ... people who love and care for me.

PAUL: What happened to us? How did we get into being so unorganized? (*Silence ... Ancestral Spiritual Council stirs about...stands, and then lean in, looking into this scene in the present*).

ELIZABETH: Perhaps all is not lost ... Who can help us? Who can we talk too? Who will listen to us?

(*All the Ancestral Spirits stage whisper ....*)

ANCESTRAL SPIRITS: THE SPIRIT

JOSEPH: I can feel a Presence in this place ... Can you feel it? Like something or someone is watching over us ... (Everyone respond in their own way) It is like a certain calmness ... spiritual ... holy ... Let us ask the Creator for the Holy Spirit to intervene into our lives and so that we can repent and turn from our contrary lives ... to get on track with what we are about.

ELIZABETH: I always felt like my Great-grandmother was watching over me. She was a strong, black woman who carried on with her children after my Great-grandfather was shot in his back by the Tenant farm owner who kept granddaddy in debt year after year. But when that old Tenant farm owner disrespected granny...granddaddy stood up to him and was shot in the back as he turned toward granny. Yes, we need not only ask forgiveness for our contrary ways but also to be lead toward being of service to our people. Like granddaddy, we need to stand up to weapons of mass destruction ... Biological, chemical and psychological warfare ... AIDS and Crack and a host of other chemicals poisoning our body systems, tearing down our community structures, and attacking us through social structures, public school mis-education, political movements and legal entanglements. IT MAKES ME WANT TO HOLLER SOMETIMES...THE WAY THEY DO MY LIFE.

MARY: Elizabeth, we, not only; as a people, attacked mentally, physically and spiritually, but our future destroyed before our children are born. What we put into our bodies, affect what goes into our reproductive system. Perhaps, that is why we were fortunate to attend college ... to really become prepared to make a difference ... as a Biology major, I can begin to do a study on the overall affects and effects of the biological and chemical environments exposed to us. Mmmmmmmm.... then we can be better able to educate our people of the effects of BIO-CHEM not only on ourselves but on our futures. Elizabeth you have given me an idea.

ELIZABETH: And Mary, as an accounting major, I am concerned with the HUGE amount of African and descendants of African people around the globe who have died and are dying as I speak and who will be dying year after year from BIO-CHEM warfare and tie that into the After-Math of our ancestors who were captured as prisoners, in their homeland, kidnapped, under dehumanizing conditions, to be seasoned, then sold as chattel. And since, this is a global phenomenon ... my economic study will attempt to answer the question...How does massive killings upon Africans and African people in the Diaspora within the last 500 hundred years been a benefit to the New World. Ooooooo ... my brain has never worked this hard before ... something within me is pushing ideas through to my brain...Paul, I have to do something...

PAUL: I can do something right now ... I can use my office as President of the Freshman Class ... Yeah ... I can "propose that we approach Student Government to elect to spread information throughout the College Body advising students of our research findings and then they can carry those findings to their homes, churches and their communities. Also, I will propose that the student representative to the Board of Trustees advise the Board of our concerns and that we invite their input through grants and proposals to fund our warfare plans to wipe out biological, chemical weapons of mass destruction from our communities.

SARAH: What about my problem, I need help? I have AIDS now and there is no cure for it. My baby will have AIDS when it is born. The father has AIDS. What are we to do? I can't stand it...l have ringing in my head...I just want to HOLLER.

ROBERT: (*Slowly speaking*) I know (*Putting his arms around her.*) I really cannot make any suggestion to any of your problems ... as a solution ... however, I realize now that I have been playing around with my life. I did not tell anybody ... but I received a letter from my grandmother ... who is dying. She wrote in her letter that she is glad to know ... that before she dies ... someone from the family is attending college ... and that she has faith in me ... that I will be successful ... (*dropping to his knees*) I dropped to my knees ... by my bedside ... and I prayed to my Creator ... to give me the strength to go on ... (*rising to his feet*)... I do not know about that can we got earlier ... but I do know that my ancestral spirits are pulling for me to endure this race ... for a purpose.

SARAH: That is what it is ... a purpose ... I have not been tested for AIDS ... yet. I was afraid to find out the inevitable. I let my mind run away with itself ... thinking of all kinds of things ... However, I am going to the clinic today. I am also going to ask my teachers to allow me to speak to every class I am allow to speak to concerning my situation ... about the dangers of AIDS and ask all students to join me in this fight against this disease and all diseases plaguing our people everywhere.

PAUL: That is right ... plaguing our people everywhere. One of my teachers lectured on the African Diaspora ... We are not only in these United States of America but we are all over Latin America ... the Caribbean ... many descendants of our ancient ancestors were carried to Brazil, Columbia, Venezuela, Peru, and a host of other areas in that vast country during the 1500s by Portuguese and Spaniards. Many of them are being affected and infested by the same diseases affecting us including being attacked from the Air, the Sea, and from on land ... an extermination mission from the land supported by Private and Government interests. When you think about it ... Elizabeth ... and you start counting the numbers ... let us not such count 22 million African Americans ... thinking only of these United States of America ... rather think of 500,000,000 African Americans in these Western Hemisphere. Then we can get a true picture of ourselves as we link up with our Bloods below the Borders ... in the Latin Quarters.

ELIZABETH: Paul please be careful. Remember, Homeland Security ... They will arrest you and hold you for revealing the truth.

ROBERT: That's it...for 500 years we have been threatened, terrorized, maimed, killed, deceived about what is and what isn't until we do not know if we are living normally or abnormally ... that's probably the reason we've been sleeping ... through biological, chemical, and psychological weapons of mass destruction ... until we do not know who is with us or against us until we have become saboteurs of self ... thinking others are harming us ... my thoughts are going into all types of directions ... but I do know one thing ... the old folks say ... TOGETHER WE STAND ... DIVIDED WE FALL.

SARAH: Well ...it is time for us to wake up ... to get up ... to stay up ... to search for the truth ... to shed light upon the truth ... Joseph you suggested ... earlier ... that we pray ... lead us in prayer now.

JOSEPH: What do I say?

MARY: The Old Folks used to Hum and Moan ... My mother said the Elders use to do that to open the door for the ancestral spirits to come through to provide comfort for them when they were terrorized by slavers and chattel owners ... the ancestral spirits would carry messages to the Holy Spirit who would intercede in their behalf (*Mary start humming an old spiritual "Steal Away"* ... *students join in* ... *some hum* ... *others moan as they sit on the floor in a semi-circle*) OMMMMM ... (*the hum begins to sound more like a moan* ... *their eyes are closed shut. Ancestral Spirits begin to move toward downstage and around students as a mist flows on stage* ... *ancestral music flows in* ... *arms stretched toward the heavens they form circles around students* ... *then small circles around students* ... *as Joseph begin to pray*). ... Harambee .... The Lord is my Shepherd. .. I shall not want...

*(Lights fade to black on Act II briefly.)*


## ACT III

## SCENE 1

## CHARACTERS
The Ancestral Spirits

**SCENE:** As light fades in, Ancient music is heard as Ancestral Spirit chant, Ka ... Ka ... Ka ... Ka. Students are in same position as at the end of Act II. Flashing light reveals dancers illuminating in and out from among Ancestral Spirits. Drumming is heard louder and louder, and then stop. All is silent for a while. Akhenaton stage cross downstage as he speaks.


AKHENATON: *(With arms raised toward the heaven)* Almighty Everlasting Creative Essence Spirit ... the Spirit that guided us toward the journey into the afterlife ... hear my voice (*Light illuminates from the right side of stage*) as I call upon you to intervene into the lives within this world. These are your seeds. These are the ones who survived the wicked wilderness (*He opens his arms and hands referring to the students*).

IMHOTEP: *(Imhotep circles the students as he speaks with arms raised)* I come in peace as your first earthy physician. Your Divine Spirit gave me the power to heal injuries and diseases. I now call upon you to spread your wings over thy people and cast their illnesses toward their perpetrators (*Imhotep uses his staff and ankh as wands as he pass over each student*).

NZINGA: *(Nzinga stage cross with dignity as she speaks drumming praise her movements*) My people you must resist the psychological impositions that has been imposed upon you and raise your thoughts toward higher purposes and diseases will leave you as you propel on your true journey (*Nzinga pass her bow and arrows over the students*).

NEFERTITI: This is not a destination for you. You must stay the course. You must realize your purpose. You must rise up and take your rightful place in society. Let us meditate upon these children of the Light that they must rise up to their occasion (*Bowelle leads the charge as music and voices shouts out the call for ... soldiers of life ... to stand*).

ANCESTRAL SPIRITS: Soldiers of Life ... must stand. Soldiers of Life ... must stand ... Soldiers of Life ... must stand

BOWELLE: (*As Bowelle struts around the stage floor, his strong voice demands evil spirits to flee from within the body of the students*) Esu, Esu, Esu ... Come forth from within the Bowels of these people and cast your lots upon the world they live in (*As Lightning and Thunder occurs, Bowelle shakes his fist toward the heavens, then with open hands raised toward the Heavens, shouts*) SHANGOOOOOO. (*He turns and all ancestral spirits remaining downstage turn with him and stride upstage toward their Council seats, as lights dims down and stand looking toward the students whose moments has been suspended*).

# ACT III

## SCENE 2

## CHARACTERS
The College Students

---

**SCENE:** As we barely see the Ancestral Spirit Council, lights slowing fades in from the sides and front focused upon the students in the student lounge. Students begin to stir about as light hits them and their prayers and meditation begins to end.

JOSEPH: (*In low, rising stage whisper*) And I shall dwell in the House of the Lord forever and ever. Harambee... Harambee...Let us pull together ... We can no longer just be individuals... we must learn to function as units ... or else die isolated and cut off from each other. We have to be like Mafundi ... Craftsmen, Huh! Wow... I felt like I was in a dream and many of our ancient ancestors were around us ... We entered into a powerful prayer and meditation. It was as if I could sense spirits moving around and about us.

MARY: Whatever occurred as we meditated happened for a reason, it has revealed a potential for us to study. I must hurry to the Biology Lab to discuss a study with my Professor. Somehow, I received an idea of how our body cells relate to our brain cells and cells passed down to us from our ancestors through our genes to protect us. I must hurry while I have this thought.

SARAH: Wait up, Mary! I am going to the clinic and get a check up to know for sure what is going on inside my body. I am no longer going to just think on things and I fall into a slump...and be down in the dumps ... For some reason it seems as though all fear is gone. I sense a spiritual movement going on inside of me ... like I have been reborn. Hum! What a wonderful sensation to have! Let's go! (*Mary and Sarah leaves*).

ROBERT: (*He stands up and he looks around, stares at Joseph, Paul and Elizabeth*) My desire was to be an NFL player. I can see now that I really had no passion to play football. I just played to get a college scholarship. Now, I sense a purpose in my life. I never had a sensation like this before. I know what Sarah means. I too have a certain quiet peace within me. It is like some spiritual field is within urging me to go forward, onward on a journey. My life is not a destination but a journey. I must use my brain ... not just my muscles... I sense a stronger desire to lead my people out from under the wilderness many of them are in ...I must continue to pray on it ... for guidance and direction for this journey by the 'Spirit'.

PAUL: My professor said on the first day of class ... that he would take us on a journey ... starting from the Land of Spirits ... a place called Het Ka ... thousands of years before the Romans called it Africa.

JOSEPH: I had that same professor, I recall him taking us on a journey from Het Ka through ancient Greece, Western Europe and on into the Western Hemisphere ... He said that eventually we would become enlighten of ourselves and this world we live in. He indicated that Ancestral Spirits are imbedded within cells in our genes. That they want to protect us and guide us along the pathways. That we would discover a purpose for our lives.

ELIZABETH: Perhaps that is what Mary discovered and why she is in a hurry to get to her Biology department. I heard something about Sickle Cell stemming from our ancient ancestors ... when something occurred within them ... that caused cells to insulate themselves from the then deadly malaria. That their offspring, as prisoners of war, were transported to this country without a major threat of malaria ... that those cells reacted. It was as the result of environmental change that affected biological reactions.

PAUL: That professor said that our ancestors paid a great deal of attention to health ... that the Father of Medicine ... Imhotep of Het Ka recognized diseases and prescribed medicine to cure his patients. It is all making sense to me now. I didn't understand it then. But since Joseph lead us into prayer and we went into meditation, I found myself listening to voices coming from deep inside of me, like revealing things to me that somehow I knew all along. I know now why I am here. I am here to become enlightened about myself and my true purpose for living. As president of the freshman class, I am going to form study groups to address those things we sense within us ... they have value ... and invite professors who can share their experiences with us and not just from book learned but from knowledge of themselves and their ancestors.

ROBERT: We can start with ourselves. From what you just said, I think that is why we allowed weapons of mass destruction to penetrate our brain, our body, and our spiritual ... because we had a void inside of us ... we needed satisfaction of any kind or from whatever source we could get. We became prison guards of ourselves; locking ourselves down ... seeking instant self-gratification ... when all the while it was the affairs of our ancestors waking up inside of us. We are who we are. We must begin to awaken our sisters and brothers all over the globe.

ELIZABETH: We have already started. (*Lights fade as clouds, lightning and thunder, with drummers and dancers praising the end of a beginning*).

(*Curtain*)

# HELP!

Help! is a storytelling of bondage, oppression and of refugees. The stage production includes "Slave Narratives" as prepared by the Federal Writers' Project of the Works Progress Administrations for the states of Texas, Florida, Alabama, Indiana, Georgia, North and South Carolina. Professor Brooks received a divine intervention during his hospitalization at the Dorn Veterans Affairs Medical Center, in Columbia, South Carolina, as a patient in severe pain, August 31, 2005. As Brooks was getting unconscious, he sought for a divine guide to lead him to Almighty God, as he understood His Spirit to be. Brooks had a conscious contact with Almighty God. It was at that time he reviewed a scene in his conscious mind, of people lost in dark murky waters in New Orleans. There were dead bodies around them and babies crying as they floated out into the dark waters of Hurricane Katrina Levee, crying for HELP! Brooks heard familiar songs sung in the background.

This scene played repeatedly in Brooks' conscious as the scene moved from ships in the Middle Passage, to hearing voices of former slaves telling their narratives, to people wading in the waters caught up in the bondage and oppression of time as refugees. It was as it time stood still as ships in the waters, carrying human cargo of people lost in the dark with dead bodies, urine, feces and afterbirth flowing around them, as the scene played out again in Ward 9, New Orleans. Brooks dedicates these works to the children missing from their parents.

Slave narratives prepared by the Federal Writers' Project of the Works Progress Administrations For the states of Texas, Florida, Alabama and Indiana, Georgia, North and South Carolina and news footage.

This presentation stems from the roots of African Theater. The storytelling is dedicated to the children still missing from their parents.

## THE PLAY

## CHARACTERS

NARRATOR: Jalai, Griot, Shaman or Storyteller

MAN IN THE WATER: New Orleans, Present

WOMAN IN THE WATER: New Orleans, Present

CHARLES W. DICKENS: Born August 16, 1861,
        North Carolina

AMIE LUMPKIN: Ex-Slave 88 Years Old, Columbia, SC

MOLLY PARKER: Had a Good Overseer Treated Slaves
        Right, Alabama

CAROLINE HOLLAND: Had Many Masters, Alabama

GABE HINES: Was Kidnapped By Carpetbaggers, Alabama

JACK CAUTHERN: Ex-Slave 85 Years Old, Texas

MARGRETT NICKERSON: Born Many Years Ago, Florida

"FATHER" CHARLES COATES: Ex-Slave 108 Years Old,
        Florida

IRENE COATES: Born 1859, Georgia, Lived In Florida

RIAS BODY: Born April 9, 1846, Georgia

PEOPLE ON ROOF TOP: Signs Calling For Help-9-1-1

DANCERS

SINGERS

MUSICIANS

REFUGEES

## SCENE

The stage is bare, as House goes to dark, with the exception of a white cyclorama upstage with black borders and a podium downstage right for the Narrator. "Kristy Love" Brooks is heard singing, her song of Hope, "It Will Be Better." A traditional African Drummer appears upstage right of the black border slightly near to the cyclorama and lightly play the drum nearing the end of "Kristy's song as stage crew(dressed in black) place Five Music Stands on each side of the stage (left and right). At this time, the stage, still dark, has a Narrator's podium downstage right, a traditional African drummer upstage right, and five V-Shaped Music Stands (Five on each side of the stage). Kristy's song ends, African drumming is heard loud and strong as LIGHTS fade in slightly as Dancers enters from stage left toward down center stage. Dance movements reveals a journey from Africa to the Caribbean, to South and North Americas, to Counterfeit Reality Time, to New Orleans, to the present LIGHTS fade out as, News footage is revealed upon the cyclorama of the event known as "Hurricane Katrina Levee." A Singer appears stage center. Images continue to play upon the cyclorama.


SINGER:
*Sometimes I Feel Like a Motherless Child*
From American Negro Spirituals
By J. W. Johnson, J. R. Johnson, 1926

Sometimes I feel like a motherless child
Sometimes I feel like a motherless child
Sometimes I feel like a motherless child
A long ways from home
A long ways from home
 A long ways from home
Along ways from home
Sometimes I feel like a motherless child
Sometimes I feel like a motherless child
Sometimes I feel like a motherless child
A long ways from home
A long ways from home
True believer
A long ways from home
Along ways from home

*(A man appears fearful from the aftermath of the "Katrina Levee" nearing the last stanza of the song downstage center LIGHTS fades in on him)*

MAN IN THE WATER:
My wife was holding on to me, in the water, my children and grandchildren were holding on to me ... my wife, she begins to let go. I say, "hold on Honey, hold on ... but she say, "take care of our children and grandchildren ... and she let go ...I seen her as she drift off into that dark, murky water ...I held on to our children and grandchildren ... but I was lost without my wife ... my friend ... my mother ... HELP! *(Woman stage crosses down center and sit on lip of stage as Lights focus on her looking out into waters at a medical boat)*.

WOMAN IN THE WATER:
*(As if talking to her five years old son)* David, you must grow up real fast, for mommy, okay, ah mum. I need for you to sit here on this dock, for me, okay, ah mum. Mommy's labor pains are coming faster now. Your sister is about to be born. *(Still looking at the boat beyond the audience)*. Once, I get to that medical boat and I give birth to your sister. I'll come back for you, okay. And if don't come back, you wait here for some person to come along and you go with them, okay, ah mum *(as mommy stretched forth her arms to dive into the waters LIGHTS fade out slowly, as Singer stands stage center singing, mommy leaves stage by way of pit toward right stage door quietly, as light fade in upon Singer)*.

SINGER:
*A Change Is Gonna Come*
By Sam Cooke, 1963

I was born by the river in a little tent
And just like that river I've been running ever since
It's been a long time coming
But I know a change is gonna come, oh yes it will
It's been too hard living, but I'm afraid to die

Cos I don't know what's out there beyond the sky
It's been a long, a long time coming
But I know a change is gonna come, oh yes it will
I go to the movie
And I go down town
Somebody keep telling me don't hang around
It's been a long time coming
But I know a change is gonna come, oh yes it will
Then I go to my brother
And I say brother help me please
But he winds up knockin' me
Back down on my knees
There were times when I thought I couldn't last for long
But now I think I'm able to carry on
It's been a long, a long time coming
But I know a change gone come, oh yes it will

PEOPLE:
(*Enter stage carrying demonstration signs, chanting*) ... EMERGENCY
RESCUE ... WHEN DO WE WANT IT...NOW...MEDICAL
ATTENTION... WHEN DO WE WANT IT
NOW...CHILDREN UNITED WITH THEIR PARENTS ...
WHEN DO WANT IT NOW, SHELTER...WHEN DO WE
WANT IT... NOW. (One big sign goes up with HELP NOW
on it). THEY LEFT US HERE TO DIE (*Narrator steps to the
podium*).

NARRATOR:
(*Lights fade in on Narrator*) They left us here 400 hundred years
to die. They took control of us when they horded us into
prisons, then chained us together as we wade into the waters to
board stinking filthy ships with the name Jesus on them
signifying Jospheus or Hesu. Our ancestors were stacked upon
five levels in the ships, including the bottom of the ships,
sailing to unknown seaports. The ships swaying back and forth
in the waters shifting filthy waste of feces, urine decaying

afterbirth, and dead bodies covering live bodies chained together to swallow these waters of waste. It was shocking to see this scene repeated during "Hurricane Katrina Levee" in New Orleans as African Americans were observed wading in waters of filth, toxin waste, feces, urine, and dead African Americans, living below sea level, in Ward Nine, in New Orleans, while they held the key to the Levees that overflowed into Ward Nine bringing Black People into the waters again ... with feces, urine, and dead bodies ... just like it was when our ancestors were chained, stacked up ill the bottom of the ship... just like Amiri Baraka describes it in his shocking play "The Slave Ship." Why must we always look to them for help ... when they have only brought GENOCIDE...Nay Sayers...remember Jim Jones ... 1975. Close to 2,000 black babies are aborted daily...figure out the Mathematics times 365 days a year. Where were you? Some of you look like you are to surprise to hear these stories ... Where are you NOW? People of Color all over the GLOBE are faced with GENOCIDE. Our BLOOD SEEPED INTO THE CARIBBEAN, MEXICO, CENTRAL AMERICA, LATIN AMERICA, NORTH AMERICA; FROM AFRICA ... TODAY WE ARE ONE HALF BILLION AFRICANS LIVING IN THE WESTERN HEMISPHERE ... THAT IS A HUGE POPULATION ... WE NO LONGER NEED TO BE SEPARATED FROM OUR BLOODLINE... Where are our children? We need to have our children with us. When we go to meetings ... They must be with us ... We need to tell our children the truth ... We need to tell them about our ancient civilization and let them read Chancellor Williams' book, The Destruction of the Black Civilization ... We must tell them about the Willie Lynch Manifesto that has black people enslaved through psycho-tropics, through post stress trauma through classical conditioning, through counterfeit media realities, that divides and separates us from each other because of symbolisms of colors. This so-called white system has never worked for us and it never will...even though we build it...it won't work...tell your children that we are a great and global people. Listen to what Katrina had to tell us...militias from across the country came to harness black people to keep them in their place while they suffered humiliation, lies and deceptions to degrade them while they sought out food, water, medicine, and fresh clothing to get out of their filthy clothing from lack of proper sanitation ... While law enforcement looted stores, shooting and killing black folks, while frightening off rescues from reaching them ... As law enforcement covered their ugly deeds by blaming innocent victims flooded out by a contaminated levee and even in the aftermath of the storm vented their nothingness by beating up an old black man, retired educator, to the ground. Are you so enslaved that you refuse to allow your brain eye to see these things for you. Laura Bush said, "The worst thing about black people in the Superdome is that they might want to stay there. William Bennett said "to get rid of crime kill all new born black babies." Let us examine by listening to the voices of those who lived and endured harsh and cruel treatment as slaves and compare them with your own thoughts and debate among yourselves how our thoughts are the same and as to how far they have or have not advanced.

*(As Jalai leaves the stage a singer or singers sing the following song. An ensemble of dancers and actors make body movements as actors and actresses assemble to places, five on each side of the stage, as dancers are down center stage, while singers are up stage center ... Lights)*

SINGER(S):

*Nobody Knows De Trouble I've Seen*
Arranged by E.T. Burleigh

Nobody knows de trouble I've seen, Nobody knows but Jesus
Nobody knows de trouble I've seen, Glory hallelujah!
Sometimes I'm up sometimes I'm down.

Oh yes, Lord! Sometimes I'm almos' to de groun';
Oh yes, Lord!
Oh nobody knows de trouble I've seen,
Nobody knows but Jesus.
Nobody knows de trouble I've seen, Glory, Hallelujah!
If you get there before I do,
Oh yes, Lord! Tell all my friends I'm coming too,
Oh yes, Lord! Oh nobody knows de trouble I've seen,
Nobody knows but Jesus.
Nobody knows de trouble I've seen,
Glory, Hallelujah.

# IRENE

FEDERAL WRITERS' PROJECT American Guide, (Negro Writers' Unit) Jacksonville, Florida
Viola B. Muse Field Worker Complete 1,143 Words
5 Pages
Slave Interview December 16, 1936

## IRENE COATES

Immediately after slavery in the United States, the southern white people found themselves without servants. Women who were accustomed to having a nurse, maid, cook and laundress found themselves without sufficient money to pay wages for all these people. There was a great amount of work to be done and the great problem confronting married women who had not been taught" to work and who thought it beneath their standing to soil their hands, found it very difficult.

There were on the other hand many Negro women who needed work and young girls who needed guidance and training. The home and guidance of the aristocratic white people offered the best opportunity for the dependent un-schooled freed women; and it was in this kind of home that the ex-slave child of this story was reared.

Irene Coates of 2015 Windle Street, Jacksonville, Florida, was born in Georgia about 1859. She was close to six years of age when freedom was declared.

She was one among the many Negro children who had the advantage of living under the direct supervision of kind whites and receiving the care which could only be excelled by an educated mother.

Jimmie and Lou Bedell were the names of the man and wife who saw the need of having a Negro girl come into their home as one in the family and at the same time be assured of a good and efficient servant in years to come.

When Irene was old enough, she became the nurse of the Bedell baby and when the family left Savannah, Georgia to come to Jacksonville, they brought Irene with them.

Although Irene was just about six years old when the Civil War ended, she has vivid recollection of happenings during slavery. Some of the incidents which happened were told her by her slave associates after slavery ended and some of them she remembers herself.

Two incidents which she considers caused respect for slaves by their masters and finally the Emancipation by Abraham Lincoln she tells in this order.

The first event tells of a young, strong healthy Negro woman who knew her work and did it well. "She would grab up two bags of guana (fertilizer) and tote 'em at one time," said Irene, and was never found shirking her work. The overseer on the plantation, was very hard on the slaves and practiced striking them across the back with a whip when he wanted to spur them on to do more work.

Irene says, one day a crowd of women were hoeing in the field and the overseer rode along and struck one of the women across the back with the whip, and the one nearest her spoke and said that if he ever struck her like that, it would be the day he or she would die. The overseer heard the remark and the first opportunity he got, he rode by the woman and struck her with the whip and started to ride on. The woman was hoeing at the time, she whirled around, struck the overseer on his head with the hoe, knocking him from his horse, she then pounced upon him and chopped his head off. She went mad for seconds and proceeded to chop and mutilate his body; that done to her satisfaction, she then killed his horse. She then calmly went to tell the master of the murder, saying, "I've done killed de overseer," the master replied, "Do you mean to say you've killed the overseer?" she answered yes, and that she had killed the horse also. Without hesitating, the master pointing to one of his small cabins on the plantation said, "You see that house over there?" she answered yes at the same time looking

"Well said he, take all your belongings and move into that house and you are free from this day and if the mistress wants you to do anything for her, do it if you want to." Irene related with much warmth the effect that incident had upon the future treatment of the slaves.

The other incident occurred in Virginia. It was upon an occasion when Mrs. Abraham Lincoln was visiting in Richmond. A woman slave owner had one of her slaves whipped in the presence of Mrs. Lincoln. It was easily noticed that the woman was an expectant mother. Mrs. Lincoln was horrified at the situation and expressed herself as being so, saying that she was going to tell the President as soon as she returned to the White House. Whether this incident had any bearing upon Mr. Lincoln's actions or not, those slaves who were present and Irene says that they all believed it to be the beginning of the President's activities to end slavery.

Besides these incidents, Irene remembers that women who were not strong and robust were given such work as sewing, weaving and minding babies. The cloth from which the Sunday clothes of the slaves was made was called ausenburg and the slave women were very proud of this. The older women were required to do most of the weaving of cloth and making shirts for the male slaves.

When an old woman who had been sick, regained her strength, she was sent to the fields the same as the younger ones. The ones who could cook and tickle the palates of her mistress and master were highly prized and were seldom if ever offered for sale at the auction block.

The slaves were given fat meat and bread made of husk of corn and wheat. This caused them to steal food and when caught they were severely whipped.

Irene recalls the practice of blowing a horn whenever a sudden rain came. The overseer had a certain Negro to blow three times and if shelter could be found, the slaves were expected to seek it until the rain ceased.

The master had sheds built at intervals on the plantation. These accommodated a goodly number; if no shed was available the slaves stood under trees. If neither was handy and the slaves got wet, they could not go to the cabins to change clothes for fear of losing time from work. This was often the case; she says that slaves were more neglected than the cattle.

Another custom which impressed the child-mind of Irene was the tying of slaves by their thumbs to a tree limb and whipping them. Women and young girls were treated the same as were men.

After the Bedells took Irene to live in their home they traveled a deal. After bringing her to Jacksonville, when Jacksonville was only a small port, they then went to Camden County, Georgia.

Irene married while in Georgia and came back to Jacksonville with her husband Charles, the year of the earthquake at Charleston, South Carolina, about 1888.
Irene and Charles Coates have lived in Jacksonville since that time. She relates many tales of happenings during the time that this city grew from a town of about four acres to its present status.

Irene is the mother of five children. She has nine grandchildren and eight great-grandchildren. Her health is fair, but her eyesight is poor. It is her delight to entertain visitors and is conversant upon matters pertaining to slavery and reconstruction days.

# GABE
## Alabama
### Gertha Couric Susan Russell, Editor

## GABE WAS KIDNAPPED
## BY CARPETBAGGERS

Old Gabe had been long in this world—close to one hundred years. He had experienced much but one incident had outlasted all the others—even the stroke that made him older and feebler. That experience had caused Gabe and his "ole woman" to stray far from the fold and to walk all the way back to its shelter.

That was back in Reconstruction days, when he was not "bandy in his knees" and long before Anna left him alone in his cabin with just memories of earlier and happier days.

Gabe was "birthed in Cusseta, Georgia" the son of two faithful old slaves, Hetty and Gabe Hines, and they "all 'longed to Marsa William Shipp an' Miss Ma'y. He told his story thus:

"Endurin' of de fiah, I was big enough to be water toter on de plantation. No, Li'l Missy, I doan 'zactly know how old I is 'ceptin' by de squeakin' an' achin' of my bones. I 'members lots 'bout doze days. Dem was happy times, Li'l Missy. Arter we all was freed, I went to Silver Run to live and dar I mahied Anna. She lef' me nine yeahs ago an' that broke the happiness. I miss her ev'whar, jes' keep a-missin' her though nine yeahs hev gone sence dey tuk her from de cabin an' lef' her up thar on de hill. Dere's nights when de mis'ry in dese ol' bones jist gits past standin' an' on sich nights she come ter me and holp me wid de linnymint jes' as she useter do. But she caint stay long when she come.

"I wuz a-tellin' 'bout Silver Run. Arter we was mahied and—gittin' use to bein' free niggahs, an' happy in our cabin, one night a gen'ultan from de no'th was to see us an' he tol' us if we'd go wid him he'd pay us big wages an' gin us a fine house to boot.

51

"Fer two nights we sot dere by dat chimbly a-thinkin' a sight to do or to don't and ponderin' this way and t'other one. Den we 'cided to go. We lef ev'ything dar 'ceptin' whut we tied up in a bandana han'chief, and we tied that onto a stick for de gen'ulnan frum de no'th wouldn't let us take no baggage. We was goin' to Columbus, Georgia but we didn't know dat.

"Li'l Missy, when we got dar, whar he was a-takin' us, we foun'the big wages to be fifty cents a month, and dat fine house tu'ned out to be mo' like a stable. Instid of our cabin and gyarden and chickens and our trees, we had a turrible place, right out under the hot sun wid watah miles away down a hill. And he wan't no gent'man from de no'th!

"Missy, I nebber will be able to tell myself whut made us do hit no mo' den I'll ebber be able to tell how skeered I wuz one night when de wind howled an' de lightnin' was sprayin' ober de-place an! de rain was so turrible hit was a-sobbin' in de fire. He knowed de debbil was ridin' de win' dat night.

"We was a-sittin! dar befo' de fire me an' my ol' woman, when we heard a stompin' like a million horses had stopped outside de do'. I tipped to de do' an' peeked out an', Li'l Missy, whut we seed was so turrible our eyes Jes' mos' popped cut our haid. Dere was a million hosses all kivered in white, wid dey eyes pokin' out and a-sittin' on de hosses was men kivered in white too, tall as giants, n' dey eyes was a-pokin' out too. Dere was a leader an' he heldt a bu'nin' cross in his hand.

"When we seed dat, we fell on our po' knees, skeered mos' to def an' we axed de Great Marster to help two po' ol' niggers an' holp 'em quick.

"De fust thing we knowed dem Ku Kluxes had de gen'man from de no'th out of his aidin' place 'hind our house an' a-settin' on one of dem hosses. Dey nebber spoke wid him. Dev ies' tuk him off somewhar, we nebber knowed whar, but he di'n't come back no mo'.

"Li'l Missy, we heard arterwards dat dis gen'lman from de no'th wuz no qual'ty a-tall. Dat he was de wu'st leadah of all de debilment bein' done; one of dem carpetbaggin' men.

"Nex' day arter de Ku Kluxes cotched dis man, his wife lef' Columbus in a hurry, sayin' she couldn't sociate wid de Columbus ladies 'caze dey was so po'. Dey was po'! Dey is no denyin' that. De was all po' caze the Yankees done ruint Columbus. But, li'l Missy, dey's a big dif'' ence in bein' po' an' qual'ty an' bein' jes po' white trash.

"What did I do then? Well, Li'l Missy, we lef'' Columbus arter whut happen'd an' we walked to Eufaula, whar twas safe to be. For forty yeahs I w'uked for de city and Anna, she tuk in Washin' Endurin' dat time we was gettin' along pretty likely, when one day Gabriel blew his horn for Anna, and Gabe was lef'' alone.

"My ol' woman's gone. Li'l Missy, mos' ev'y one I knowed is dead. Dis heah cabin ain' home to me no mo'. Hits lonely ev'y whar. Maybe I'd orter be thinkin' 'bout Canaan, but hits ol' times crowds dis ol' darkey's heart. Li'l Missy, may be whin I gits to whar Anna is hit will be ol' times all ovah ag'in."

# AMIE

Project #1655, Stiles M. Boruggs, Columbia, S. C.

## AMIE LUMPKIN
## EX-SLAVE 88 YEARS OLD

"I was born on de plantation of Master John Mobley, in Fairfield County, South Carolina, in 1849. Both my parents was slaves on that plantation at that time. Master Mobley had a big farm and he had many slaves and chillum when I began to understand things there. My daddy worked in de field, but my mammy worked in de big house, helpin' to cook."

"There was pretty good order on de plantation, generally at de time in 1856, when I was 'bout seven years old. Most of de slaves go right along doin' their chores, as expected of them, but a few was restless, and they break de rules, by runnin' 'bout without askin,' and always there was one or two who tried to escape slavery by goin' far away to the North."

"I 'member seein' one big black man, who tried to steal a boat ride from Charleston. He stole away one night from Master Mobley's place and got to Charleston, befo' he was caught up with. He toll the overseer who questioned him after he was brought back: "Sho' I try to git away from this sort of thing. I was goin' to Massachusetts, and hire out 'til I git 'nough to carry me to my home in Africa."

"It was de rule when a trial was bein' held lak this, for all de bosses and sometimes de missus to be there to listen and to ask the

run'way slave some questions." After this one talked, it was Missus Mobley herself who said: "Put yourself in this slave's shoes, and what would you do? Just such as he has. The best way to treat such a slave is to be so kind and patient with him, that he will forget his old home."

"He was led away and I never did hear if he was whipped. He lak a Cherokee Indian, he never whisper if he should be whipped 'til de blood stream from him; but I do know he never got away again. He was de first one to pick up his hat and laugh loud, when President Lincoln set all slaves free in January, 1863; He say: Now I go, thank de Lord, and he strike right out, but he not git much beyond de barn, when he turn and come back. He walked in de yard of de big house, and he see Missus Mobley lookin' out at him. He take off his hat and bow low and say.

"Missus, I so happy to be free, that I forgits myself but I not go 'til you say so. I not leave you when you needs a hand, 'less de master and all de white folks gits home to look after you."

"De missus look down at her feet and she see de black man, so big and strong, sheddin' tears. She say to him: 'You is a good nigger and you has suffered much; make yourself at home, just as you have been doin' and when you want to go far away, come to me and I'll see that you git 'nough money to pay your way to Boston and maybe to Africa.' And that is what happen' a year or two later.

"My daddy go 'way to de war 'bout this time, and my mammy and me stay in our cabin alone. She cry and wonder where he be, if he is well, or he be killed, and one day we hear he is dead. My mammy, too, pass in a short time. I was sixteen when Sher-man's army come through Fairfield County. I see them ridin' by for hours, some of them laughin' and many of them has big balls in their hands, which they throw against de house and it explode and burn de house.

"I have always 'spected that am just de way they set de houses when Columbia was burned in a single night. Some of de houses in Fairfield was burned, some in Winnsboro, and others in de country, but Columbia was de only place that was wiped out. As de army pass, we all stand by de side of de road and cry and ask them not to burn our white folks' house, and they didn't."

I came to Columbia in 1868, and for a time I cooked in one or two of de hotels, then running in Columbia. About 1878,

I was employed as cook in de home of de late W. A. Clark, and I stayed there, in de servant's quarters, on de place 'til I became too feeble to continue.

"It has been one of de big pleasures of my life that I has so many fine white friends, and so far as I knows, de good will of all de black folks as well. While workin' at Mr. Clark's home, which stood in a fine grove of magnolias at the comer of Elmwood Avenue and Park Street I never thought I should live to see it fade away. But you know it did, since de big stone mansion was torn away and de Junior High School now stands in that grove."

"While there, I think it was about thirty years service, I saw many of de leading white folks of de city and state, as guests there; they, at least many of them, still befriend me. Do remnants of de Clark family treat me fine when they see me, and sometimes they drive by to see me. Of course, I had a pretty nice little roll of money when I got too old to work reg'larly but it has all been spent since." One day I's thinkin' 'bout it and I recalls de sayin' of my Missus Mobley. She say: "Money has wings and it soon flyaway."

"For de last twelve years now, I has been de guest of Missus Ruth Neal, a fine Christian woman and a teacher in de public schools. She always treat me just as though I be her mother. My white friends have not forget me to date and they enable me to live, without too much aid from my present benefactor. Her chillun, all in school now, call me 'Auntie.' "__ 'over my life it seems to me, I has done de best I could to live right and I have a hope that when de summons comes my Lord will say: "Well done, Amie."

(Address - Amie Lumpkin, 1411 Pine St. Columbia, S. C.)

# CHARLES

## CHARLES W. DICKENS
### 1115 East Lenoir Street

"My name is Charles W. Dickens. I lives at 1115 East Lenoir Street, Raleigh, North Carolina, Wake County. I wuz born August 16, 1861, de year de war started. My mother wuz named Ferebee Dickens. My father wuz named John Dickens. I had nine sisters and brothers. My brothers were named Alan, Douglas, my name, Jake, Johnnie and Jones. The girls Katie, Katilda, Francis, and Emily Dickens."

"My grandmother wuz named Charity Dickens. My grandfather wuz Dudley T. Dickens. I do not know where dey came from. No, I don't think I do. My mother belonged to Washington Scarborough, and so did we chilluns. My father he belonged to Obediah Dickens and missus wuz named Silvia Dickens. Dey lowed mother to go by the name of my father after dey wuz married."

"We lived in log houses and we had bunks in 'em. Master died, but I 'member missus wuz mighty good to us. We had tolerable fair food, and as fur as I know she wuz good to us in every way. We had good clothing made in a loom, that is de cloth wuz made in de loom. My father lived in Franklin County. My mother lived in Wake County. I 'member hearin' father talk about walkin' so fur to see us. There wuz about one dozen slaves on de plantation. Dere were no hired overseers. Missus done her own bossing. I have heard my father speak about de patterollers, but I never seed none. I heard him say he could not leave the plantation without a strip o' something."

"No, sir, the white folks did not teach us to read and write. My mother and father, no sir, they didn't have any books of any kind. We went to white folk's church. My father split slats and made baskets to sell. He said his master let him have all de money he made sellin' de things he made. He learned a trade. He wuz a carpenter. One of the young masters got after father, so he told me, and he went under de house to keep him from whuppin' him. When missus come home she wouldn't let young master whup him. She jist wouldn't' 'low it."

"I 'members de Yankees comin' through. When mother heard they were comin', she took us chillun and carried us down into an ole field, and after that she carried us back to the house." Missus lived in a two-story house. We lived in a little log house in front of missus' house. My mother had a shoulder of meat and she hid it under a mattress in the house. When the Yankees lef, she looked for it; they had stole the meat and gone. Yes, they stole from us slaves. The road the Yankees wuz travellin' wuz as thick wid 'em as your fingers. I 'member their blue clothes, their blue caps. De chickens they were carrying on their horses wuz crowing. Dey wuz driving cows, hogs, and things. Yes sir, ahead of 'em they come first. The barns and lots were on one side de road dey were trabellin' on and de houses on de other. Atter many Yankees had passed dey put a bodyguard at de door of de great house, and didn't 'low no one to go in dere. I looked down at de Yankees and spit at 'em. Mother snatched me back, and said, 'Come back here chile, dey will kill you.'

"Dey carried de horses off de plantation and de meat from missus' smokehouse and buried it. My uncle, Louis Scarborough, stayed wid de horses. He is livin' yet, he is over a hundred years old." He lives down at Moores Mill, Lake County, near Youngsville. Before de surrender one of de boys and my uncle got to fightin', one of de Scarborough boys and him. My uncle threw him down. The young Master Scarborough jumped up, and got his knife and cut uncle's entrails but so uncle had to carry 'em to de house in his hands. About a year after de war my father carried us to Franklin County. He carried us on a steer cart. Dat's about all I 'member about de war.

"Abraham Lincoln wuz de man who set us free. I think he wuz a mighty good man. He done so much for de colored race, but what he done was intended through de higher power.

I don't think slavery wuz right."

"I think Mr. Roosevelt is a fine man, one of the best presidents in the world. I voted for him, and I would vote for him ag'in. He has done a lot for de people, and is still doin'. He got a lot of sympathy for 'em. Yas sir, a lot of sympathy for de people."

# MOLLY

Preston Klein
Opelika, Alabama.

## HE WAS A GOOD OVERSEER AND TREATED SLAVES RIGHT

Down in lower Lee County I found Molly Parker, an old acquaintance, ailing and with the wandering mind of the aged. She could find answers to some of my questions, but some she couldn't get straight. She was just as clean and neat as she had always been, clad in an apron dress that she would call a "Mother Huggard."

Molly is eighty-five years old and lives with her sister Edna in a simple cabin, with a little patch of flowers between it and the field where Edna is still young enough to work. Molly was a housewife's treasure in the days gone by, but now she is too feeble to do more than work her little patch of flowers.

She was born in Virginia but was brought to Alabama when a child and sold to a Mr. Dunn, near Salem. Her mother and father were John and Fanny, the parents of four children, Molly, Edna, San and Albert.

"I was a big size housegirl, but I sho' could work," Molly recalled, "Mr. Digby blowed a big bugle early every morning to get us all up and going by bright light. Mr. Digby was a good overseer and treated all de slaves de best he knew how.

"I married Dick Parker on a Sunday and dey fixed us a bit dinner wid more good things to eat, but I was too happy to eat much myself. I ain't had no chillun of my own, but I hoped mammy with hern."

"De Yankees done camped nigh our house, and I had to help cook and tote de grub down to 'em. Us read in de free paper 'bout us being free. Massa didn't tell us nothing, but us stayed on for a long time atter dat. Massa had a passel of slaves.

"Yes'm, I'se a member of de church. Why I jined? Jest for protection, I reckon."

"I'd hate to see slavery time ag'in, 'cause hit sho' was bad for some of de niggers, but us fared good though."

# RIAS

## J. R Jones

## RIAS BODY, EX-SLAVE.

Place of birth:   Harris County, near Waverly Hall, Georgia
Date of birth:   April 9, 1846
Present residence: 1419 - 24th Street, Columbus, Georgia
Interviewed:   July 24, 1936

Rias Body was born the slave property of Mr. Ben Body, a Harris County planter. He states that he was about fifteen years old when the Civil War started and, many years ago, his old time white folks told him that April 9, 1846, was the date of his birth.

The "patarolers," according to "Uncle" Rias, were always quite active in antebellum days. The regular patrol consisted of six men who rode nightly, different planters and overseers taking turns about to do patrol duty in each militia district in the County.

All slaves were required to procure passes from their owners or their plantation overseers before they could go visiting or leave their home premises.

If the "patarolers" caught a "Nigger" without a pass, they whipped him and sent him home. Sometimes, however, if the "Nigger" didn't run and told a straight story, he was let off with a lecture and a warning. Slave children, though early taught to make themselves useful, had lots of time for playing and frolicking with the white children.

Rias was a great hand to go seining with a certain clique of white boys, who always gave him a generous or better than equal share of the fish caught.

At Christmas, every slave on the Body plantation received a present. The Negro children received candy, raisins and "nigger-toes," balls, marbles, etc.

As for food, the slaves had, with the exception of "fancy trimmins," about the same food that the whites ate. No darky in Harris County that he ever heard of ever went hungry or suffered for clothes until after freedom.

Every Saturday was a wash day. The clothes and bed linen of all Whites and Blacks went into wash every Saturday. And "Niggers," whether they liked it or not, had to "scrub" themselves every Saturday night.

The usual laundry and toilet soap was a home-made lye product, some of it a soft- solid, and some as liquid as water. The latter was stored in jugs and demijohns, Either would "fetch the dirt, or take the hide off"; in short, when applied "with rag and water, something had to come"

Many of the Body slaves had wives and husbands living on other plantations and belonging to other planters. As a courtesy to the principals of such matrimonial alliances, their owners furnished the men passes permitting them to visit their wives once or twice a week. Children born to such unions were the property of the wife's owner; the father's owner had no claim to them whatsoever.

"Uncle" Rias used to frequently come to Columbus with his master before the war, where he often saw "Niggers oxioned off" at the old slave mart which was located at what is now 1225 Broadway. Negroes to be offered for sale were driven to Columbus in droves—like cattle—by "Nawthon speckulatahs".

Rias Body had twelve brothers, eight of whom were "big buck Niggers," and older than himself. The planters and "patarolers" accorded these "big Niggers" unusual privileges— to the end that he estimates that they" wus de daddies uv least a hunnert head! o' chillun in Harris County before de war broke out."

And prospective buyers would visit the "block" accompanied by doctors, who would feel of, thump, and examine the "Nigger" to see if sound. A young or middle-aged Negro man, specially or even well trained in some trade or out-of-the-ordinary line of work, often sold for from $2000.00 to $4000.00 in gold. Women and "runty Nigger men" commanded a price of from $600.00 up, each. A good 'breedin' though, says "Uncle" Rias, would sometimes sell for as high as $1200.00.

Some of these children were "scattered" over a wide area. Sin, according to Rias Body, who voices the sentiment of the great majority of aged Negroes, is that, or everything, which one does and says "not in the name of the Master".

The holy command, "Whatever ye do, do it in My Name," is subjected to some very unorthodox interpretations by many members of the colored race. Indeed, by their peculiar interpretation of this command, it is established that "two clean sheets can't smut" which means that a devout man and woman may indulge in the primal passion without committing sin.

The old man rather boasts of the fact that he received a number of whippings when a slave: says he now knows that he deserved them, "an thout 'em", he would have no doubt "been hung 'fore he wuz thutty years ole."

Among the very old slaves whom he knew as a boy were quite a few whom the Negroes looked up to, respected, and feared as witches, wizards, and magic-workers. These either brought their "leamin" with them from Africa or absorbed it from their immediate African forebears. Mentally, these people wern't brilliant, but highly sensitized, and Rias gave "all sich" as wide a berth as opportunity permitted him, though he knows "dat dey had secret doins an carrying-ons". In truth, had the Southern Whites not curbed the mumbo-jumboism of his people, he is of the opinion that it would not now be safe to step "out his doe at night".

Incidentally, Rias Body is more fond of rabbit than any other meat "in de wurrul", and says that he could-if he were able to get them —eat three rabbits a day, 365 days in the year, and two for breakfast on Christmas morning. He also states that pork, though killed in the hottest of July weather, will not spoil if it is packed down in shucked corn-on-the-cob. This he learned in slavery days when, as a "run-away", he "knocked a shoat in the head" one summer and tried it— proving it.

# CAROLINE

Mabel Farrior,
Lois Lynn,
John Morgan Smith,

## CAROLINE HOLLAND HAD MANY MASTERS.

"Yassuh, I wuz a slave," spoke Aunt Carry from her vine-shaded porch at No. 3 Sharpe Street, Montgomery, Alabama. "I wuz borned in 1849 on Mr. Will Wright's plantation on the Mt. Meigs road. Massa Will had a big slave house an' us niggers sho' use to have a good time playin' 'roun' down at de slave quarters. We had a row of houses two stories high, an' dey wuz filled wid all sorts of niggers. When I wuz twelve year old, I wuz made nu'ss fer my rnistis's little girl an' at de fus' I couldn't do nothin' but rock de cradle. I didn't know how to hol' baby. Us niggers had gardeens (guardians) dat look 'atter as lak dey did atter de hosses and cows and pigs.

"One night atter we had all gone to bed I heered a noise at de window, an' when I look up dere wuz a man a climbin' in. He wuz a nigger. I could tell eben do I could scarce see him, I knowed he wuz a nigger. I could hear my mistis a breathin', an' de baby wuz soun' asleep too. I started to yell out but I thought dat de nigger would kill us so I jes' kep' quiet. He come in de window, an' he see us a sleepin' dere, an' all of a sudden I knowed who it wuz. 'Jade,' I whispers, 'What you a doin' here?' He come to my bed and put his rough han' ober my mouf.

"Listen you black pickaninny, you tell em dat you saw me here an' I'll kill you, 'he say,' I th'ow yo' hide to de snakes in de swamp. Now shet up."

"Wid dat he went to de dresser an' taken mistis' money bag. Atter dat he went to de window an' climb down de ladder an' I didn't do nothin' but shake myself nearly to death fum fright. De nex' day de oberseer an' de pattyrollers went a searchin' th'ough de slave quarters an' dey foun' de money bag under Jade's cot. Dey tuk him an' whupped him for near fifteen minutes. We could hear him holla way up at de big house. Jade, he neber got ober dat whuppin'. He died three days later. He wuz a good nigger, 'peer to me lak, an' de bes' blacksmith in de whole county. I ke'pa-wonderin' whut made him want ter steal dat purse. Den I foun' out later dat he wuz a goin' to pay a white man ter carry him ober de line to de No'thern States. Jade jus' had too big ideas fo' a nigger. I us'ta see Jade's ghos' a walkin' out in de garden in de moonlight; sometime  he sit on de fence an' look at his ole cabin, den sometimes he stroll off down de cotton fiel'. When de Lawd git th' ough a punishin' him fo' a stealin' dat money, I guess he won't make us no mo' visits. He jus' go right on in heaben. Dat's what ghos'tes is, you know; peoples dat can't quite git in heaben, an' dey hadda stroll 'roun' little longer on de outside repentin'.

"Soon after dat my gardeen tuk me to Tallasee when de massa died. My gardeen wuz a good man. He wuz always a-makin' speeches fo' de slaves to stay under bondage till dey wuz twenty-one. One dey be wuz in front of a sto' talkin' 'bout de slaves an' a man come up to him an' said he don't like de way Capt. Clanton talk (dat wuz my gardeen's name). Capt. Clanton ask him whut he goin' ter do 'bout it an' de man tuk out a pistol an' kil't de Cap'n raght dere on de spot.

"Den I wuz sold to another man, a Mr. Williamson, 'bout de time de war broke loose, an' Massa Williamson tuk me ober ter lib wid some mo' peoples. He said he had mo' slaves dan he could take keer of. Dis wuz de Abernathy plantation. While de massa wuz a standin' in de slave quarters a takin' to Mr. Abernathy, I noticed a boy wid a bad eye. I didn't lak him at all an' I tol' de rnassa I don't wanna stay, kaze I didn't lak de way dat boy Lum wid de bad eye looked at me. Den Mr. Abernathy brung up a boy 'bout sebenteen year old; a big strong lookin' boy named Jeff. He say "Jeff, look out after Carry here. Don't let her git into no trouble.' Fun dat time on till 'bout five year ago, Jeff be always look after me, kaze atter de war I ma'ied him. Now I ain't got nobody but myself.

# "FATHER" CHARLES COATES

## FEDERAL WRITERS' PROJECT
American Guide,
(Negro Writers' Unit)
Jacksonville, Florida

Viola B. Muse
Field Worker
Complete
1,888 Words
8 Pages

Slave Interview
December 3, 1936

## "FATHER" CHARLES COATES

Father Charles Coates, as he is called by all who know him, was born a slave, 108 years ago at Richmond, Virginia, on the plantation of a man named L'Angle. His early boyhood days was spent on the L'Angle place filled with duties such as minding hogs, cows, bringing in wood and such light work. His wearing apparel consisted of one garment, a shirt made to reach below the knees and with three quarter sleeves. He wore no shoes until he was a man past 20 years of age.

The single garment was worn summer and winter alike and the change in the weather did not cause an extra amount of clothes to be furnished for the slaves. They were required to move about so fast at work that the heat from the body was sufficient to keep them warm.

When Charles was still a young man Mr. L'Angle sold him on time payment to W.B. Hall; who several years before the Civil War moved from Richmond to Washington County, Georgia, carrying 135 grown slaves and many children.

Mr. Hall made Charles his carriage driver, which kept

him from hard labor. Other slaves on the plantation performed such duties as rail splitting, digging up trees by the roots and other hard work.

Charles Coates remembers vividly the cruelties practiced on the Hall plantation. His duty was to see that all the slaves reported to
work on time. The bell was rung at 5:30 a.m. by one of the slaves.

Charles had the ringing of the bell for three years; this was in addition to the carriage driving. He tells with laughter how the slaves would "grab a piece of meat and bread and run to the field" as no time was allowed to sit and eat breakfast. This was a very different way from that of the master he had before, as Mr. L'Angle was much better to his slaves.

Mr. Hall was different in many ways from Mr. L'Angle, "He was always pretending" says Charles that he did not want his slaves beaten unmercifully. Charles being close to Mr. Hall during work hours had opportunity to see and hear much about what was going on at the plantation. And he believes that Mr. Hall knew just how the overseer dealt with the slaves.

On the Hall plantation there was a contraption similar to a gallows, where the slaves were suspended and whipped. At the top of this device were blocks of wood with chains run through holes and high enough that a slave when tied to the chains by his fingers would barely touch the ground with his toes. This was done so that the slave could not shout or twist his body while being whipped. The whipping was prolonged until the body of the slave was covered with welts and blood trickled down his naked body.

Women were treated in the same manner, and a pregnant woman received no more leniency than did a man. Very often after a severe flogging a slave's body was treated to a bath of water containing salt and pepper so that the pain would be more lasting and aggravated. The whipping was done with sticks and a whip called the "cat o' nine tails," meaning every lick meant nine. The "cat o' nine tails" was a whip of nine straps attached to a stick; the straps were perforated so that everywhere the hole in the strap fell on the flesh a blister was left.

The treatment given by the overseer was very terrifying. He relates how a slave was put in a room and locked up for two and three days at a time without water or food, because the overseer thought he hadn't done enough work in a given time.

Another offense which brought forth severe punishment was that of crossing the road to another plantation. A whipping was given and very often a slave was put on starvation for a few days.

One privilege given slaves on the plantation was appreciated by all and that was the opportunity to hear the word of God. The white people gathered in log and sometimes frame churches and the
slaves were permitted to sit about the church yard on wagons and on the ground and listen to the preaching. When the slaves wanted to hold church they had to get special permission from the master, and at that time a slave hut was used. A white preacher was called in and he would preach to them not to steal, lie or run away and "be sure and git all dem weeds outen dat corn in de field and your master will think a heap of you." Charles does not remember anything else the preacher told them about God. They learned more about God when they sat outside the church waiting to drive their masters and family back home.

Charles relates an incident of a slave named Sambo who thought himself very smart and who courted the favor of the master. The neighboring slaves screamed so loudly while being whipped that Sambo told his master that he knew how to make a contraption which, if a slave was put into while being whipped would prevent him from making a noise. The device was made of two blocks of wood cut to fit the head and could be fastened around the neck tightly. When the head was put in, the upper and lower parts were clamped together around the neck so that the slave could not scream. The same effect as choking. The stomach of the victim was placed over a barrel which allowed freedom of movement. When the lash was administered and the slave wiggled, the barrel moved.

Now it so happened that Sambo was the first to be put into his own invention for a whipping. The overseer applied the lash rather heavily and Sambo was compelled to wiggle his body to relieve his feelings. In wiggling the barrel under his stomach rolled a bit straining Sambo's neck and breaking it. After Sambo died from his neck being broken the master discontinued the use of the device, as he saw the loss of property in the death of slaves.

MARGRETT

FEDERAL WRITERS' PROJECT
American Guide,
(Negro Writers' Unit)
Jacksonville, Florida

Rachel A. Austin
Field Worker
Complete
2,066 Words
8 Pages

Slave Interview
December 5, 1936

## MARGRETT NICKERSON

In her own vernacular, Margrett Nickerson was "born to William A. Carr, on his plantation near Jackson, Leon County, many years ago."

When questioned concerning her life on this plantation, she continues: "Now honey, it's been so long ago, I don' 'member ev'ything, but I will tell you whut I kin as near right as possible; I kin 'member five of Marse Carr's chillun; Florida, Susan, 'Lijah, Willie and Tom; cose Carr never 'lowed us to have a piece of paper in our hands."

"Mr. Kilgo was de fust overseer I 'member; I was big enough to tote meat an' stuff frum de smokehouse to de kitchen and to tote water in and git wood for granny to cook de dinner and fur de suckers who nu'sed de babies, an' I carried dinners back to de hands."

"On dis plantation dere was 'bout a hundred head; cookin' was done in de fireplace in iron pots and de meals was plenty of pea, greens, cornbread burnt co'n for coffee - often de marster bought some coffee fur us; we got water frum de open well. Jes 'fore de big fun fiahed dey fotched my pa frum de bay whar he was makin' salt; he had heard dem say 'de Yankees is coming and wuz so glad.''

"Dere wuz rice, cotton, co'n, tater fields to be tonded to, and cowhides to be tanned, thread to be spinned, and thread was made into ropes for plow lines."

"Ole Marse Carr fed us, but he did not care what an' whar, jes so you made dat money and when yo' made five and six bales o' cotton, said: 'Yo' ain don' nuthin.'"

"When de big fun fiahed on a Sattidy me and Cabe and Minnie Howard wuz settin' up co'n fur de plowers to come 'long and put dirt to 'em—Carr read de free papers to us on Sunday and de co'n and cotton had to be tended to—he tole us he wuz goin' to gi' us de net proceeds (here she shuckles), what turned out to be de co'n and cotton stalks. Den he asked dem what would stay wid him to step off on de right and dem dat wuz leavin' to step off on de left."

"My pa made soap frum ashes when cleaning new ground - he took a hopper to put de ashes in, made a little stoll side de house put de ashes in and po'red water on it to drip; at night after gittin' off frum work he'd put in de grease and make de soap - I made it sometime and I made it now, myself."

"My step-pa useter make shoes frum cowhides fur de farm han's on de plantation and fur eve'body on de plantation 'cept ole Marse and his fambly; dey's wuz diffunt, fine.''

"My grandma wus Pheobie Austin—my mother wuz name Rachel Jackson and my pa was name Edmund Jackson; my mother and uncle Robert and Joe wus stol' frum Virginia and fetched here. I don' know no niggers dat 'listed in de war; I don' 'member much 'bout de war only when de started talkin 'bout drillin' men fur de war, Joe Sanders was a lieutenant. Marse Carr's sons, Tom and Willie went to de war."

"We didn' had no doctors, only de grannies; we mos'ly used hippecat (ipecac) fur medicine."

"As I said, Kilgo wus de fust overseer I ricollec', then Sanders was nex' and Joe Sanders after him; John C. Haywood came in after Sanders and when de big gun fiahed old man Brookington wus dere. I never saw a nigger sold, but dey carried dem frum our house and I never see 'em no mo.'"

"We had church wid de white preachers and dey tole us to mind our masters and missus and we would be saved; if not, dey said we wouldn'. Dey never tole us nothin' 'bout Jesus. On Sunday after workin' hard all de week dey would lay down to sleep and be so tired; soon ez yo' git sleep, de overseer would come an' wake you up an' make you go to church."

"When de big gun fiahed old man Carr had six sacks uf confederate money whut he wuz carryin wid him to Athens, Georgia an' all de time if any of us gals whar he wuz an' ax him 'Marse please gi us some money' (here she raises her voice to a high, pitiful tone) he says 'I aint got a cent' and right den he would have a chis so full it would take a whol' passle uv slaves to move it. He had plenty corn, taters, pum'kins, hogs, cows ev'ything, but he didn' gi us nothin but strong pain close and plenty to eat; we slept in ole common beds and my pa made up little cribs and put hay in dem fur de chillun."

"Now ef you wanted to keep in wid Marster Carr don' drap you shoes in de field and leave 'em-- he'd beat you; you mus' tote you' shoes frum one field to de tother, didn' a dog ud be bettern you." He'd say 'You gun-haided devil, drappin' you' shoes an eve'thin' over de field.'"

"Now jes lis'en, I wanna tell you all I kin, but I wants to tell it right; wait now, I don' wanna make no mistakes and I don' wanna lie on nobody— I ain' mad now an I know taint no use to lie, I takin' my time. I done prayed an' got all de malice out o' my heart and I ain' gonna tell no lie fer um and I ain' gonna tell no lie on um. I ain' never seed no slaves sold by Marster Carr, he wuz allus tellin' me he wuz gonna sell me but he never did— he sold my pa's fust wife though."

"Dere wuz Uncle George Bull, he could read and write and, chile, de white folks didn't lak no nigger whut could read and write. Carr's wife Miss Jane useter teach us Sunday School but she did not 'low us to tech a book wid us hands. So dey useter jes take uncle George Bull and beat him fur nothin; dey would beat him and take him to de lake and put him on a log and shev him in de lake, but he always swimmed out. When dey didn' do dat dey would beat him tel de blood run outen him and den trow him back in de ditch in de field and kivver him up wid dirt, head and ears and den stick a stick up at his haid. I wuz a water toter and had stood and seen um do him dat way more'n once and I stood and looked at um tel dey went 'way to de other rows and den I grabbed de dirt ofen him and he'd bresh de dirt off and say 'tank yo,' git his hoe and go back to work. Dey beat him lak dat and he didn' do a thin' to git dat sort of treatment."

"I had a sister name Lytie Holly who didn' stand back on non' uv em; when dey'd git behin' her, she'd git behin' dem; she was dat stubbo'n and when dey would beat her she wouldn' holler and jes take it and go on. I got some whuppin's wid strops but I wanter tell you why I am cripple today:

"I had to tote tater vines on my haid, me and Fred'rick and de han's would be callin fur em all over de field, but you know honey, de two of us could' git to all uv um at once, so Joe Sanders would hurry us up by beatin' us with straps and sticks and run us all over de tater ridge; he cripple us both up and den we couldn' git to all uv em. At night my pa would try to fix me up cose I had to go back to work nex' day. I never walk straight frum dat day to dis and I have to set here in dis chair now, but I don' feel mad none now. I feel good and wants to go to he'ven. I ain't gonna tel no lie on white nor black cose taint no use."

# JACK

## EX-SLAVE STORIES (Texas)

JACK CAUTHERN, 85, was born near Austin, Texas. Dick Townes owned Jack and his parents. After they were freed, the family stayed on the plantation, but Jack went to San Angelo, because "times was too dull in Travis County."

"My master was Dick Townes and my folks come with him from Alabama. He owned a big plantation fifteen miles from Austin and worked lots of slaves. We had the best master in the whole county, and everybody called us 'Townes ' free niggers," he was so good to us, and we worked hard for him, raisin' cotton and corn and wheat and oats.

"Most the slaves lived in two-room log cabins with dirt floors, over in the quarters, but I lived in master's yard. That's where I was born. There was a tall fence 'tween the yard and the quarters and the other nigger boys was so jealous of me they wouldn't let me cross that fence into the quarters. They told me I thinked I was white, jes' for livin' in master's yard.

"Me and young master had the good times. He was nigh my age and we'd steal chickens from Old Miss and go down in the orchard and barbecus 'em. One time she cotched us and sho' wore us out! She'd send us to pick peas, but few peas we picked!

"Old Miss was good to her cullud folks. When she'd hear a baby cryin' in the night she'd put on boots and take her lantern and go see about it. If we needed a doctor she'd send for old Dr. Rector and when I had the measles he give me some pills big as the end of my finger.

"We went to church all the time. Young Miss come over Sunday mornin' and fetched all us chillen to the house and read the Bible to us. She was kind of a old maid and that was her pleasure. We had baptisin's, too. One old cullud man was a preacher. Lawd, Lawd, we had shoutin' at them camp meetin's!

"I guess we was glad to be free. Old master done die and Old Miss was managin' the plantation. She had the whole bunch in the yard and read the freedom paper. The old slaves knowed what it meant, but us young ones didn't. She told everybody they could stay and work on shares and most of 'em did, but some went back to they old homes in Alabama.

"I stayed a while and married, and came to San Angelo. The reason I come, times was dull in Travis County and I done hear so much talk 'bout this town I said I was comin' and see for myself. That was in 1900 and it was jes' a forest here then. I worked eighteen years in McCloskey's saloon, and he gave me ten dollars every Christmas 'sides my pay and a suit every year. I wish he was livin' now. My wife and I was together fifty-two years and then she died. After a long time I married again, and my wife is out pickin' cotton now.

"It seem mighty hard to me now by side of old times, but I don't know if it was any better in slavery days. "It seems mighty hard though, since I'm old and can't work."

*(There is stillness for a moment and LIGHTS fades out then fades in on Jalai)*

NARRATOR:
There are some things you must begin to do; first you must organize yourselves; you must be well informed about everything; you must not become misguided ... Everybody means well is not well intended for your well being; you must not continue to sit still and listen to how they are planning genocide upon you; you must start planning politically, communally, globally, and unity for war; over 500 hundred black prisoners in New Orleans are missing; 4000 children separated
from their families are missing; remember the three star general who commanded the militias to "turn your weapon down ... Point them down ... These are our people ... They are Americans." I watched how the white men and women were aiming their weapons at black people. Take a lesson from the ex-slaves who you heard give they on account of their lives ... How they always talk about moving on ... We are referred to as refugees ... We do not have a home ... Land ... Security. Those old ex-slaves are dead now ... Yet they prayed out there in that yard for the generations to come ... You are that generation ... So step...*(Singer(s) sings ... Dancers enters ... Ensemble forms ... Then silently turn and walk off stage).*

*Bridge Over Troubled Water*
Words and Music by Paul Simon, 1969

When you're weary, feeling small,
When tears are in your eyes
I will dry them all
I'm on your side
When times get rough
And friends just can't be found
Like a bridge over troubled water
I will lay me down
Like a bridge over troubled water
I will lay me down

When you're down and out

When you're on the street
When evening falls so hard
I will comfort you
I'll take your part
When darkness comes
And pain is all around
Like a bridge over troubled water
I will lay me down
Like a bridge over troubled water
I will lay me down

Sail on, silver girl
Sail on by
Your time has come to shine
All your dreams are on their way
See how they shine
If you need a friend
I'm sailing right behind
Like a bridge over troubled water
I will ease your mind
Like a bridge over troubled water
I will ease your mind

## Suggested Reading for Students

Brown, William Wells. "Escape; or, A Leap for Freedom: A Drama, in Five Acts." Boston: RF. Wallcut, 1858. The first play written by an African in America. A protest piece, it was used by abolitionists in their efforts to end slavery.

Hughes, Langston. "Don't You Want to be Free?"** James Weldon Johnson Collection, Beinecke Rare Book and Manuscript Library Yale University. 1938. Revised 1963. A history play.

Lamb, Wendy. ed. "Sparks in the Park and Other Plays from the 1987 and 1988 Foundations of the Dramatists Guild Young Playwrights Festivals." New York, Laurel Leaf Books, 1989. Anthology of award winning plays written by teenagers.

Mutwa, Vusamazulu Credo. "Indaba, My Children." London, Stanmore Press, 1966. The oral history of the Bantu of South Africa as recorded by Vusamazulu Credo Mutwa a "Guardian of the Umalando or Tribal History."

# SHELTER

SHELTER is the place where people find refuge from the storms of life. Many have come to the end of the road; there is nowhere else to go and no one else to turn to, so they seek the SHELTER.

When men and women are faced with tough decisions and difficult issues, it is hard to understand that there is a solution. Many feel life has dealt them a wrong hand and they are hurting. Some even feel abused and let down by family, friends, and society.

SHELTER offers those who have lost hope a sense of comfort and belonging. SHELTER is a place where lives are transformed with a newness of mind, soul, and spirit.

SHELTER offers people an awakening that redirects their broken lives on a clear path where they find support among each other. It is at this point in their lives that spirituality comes forth.

# THE PLAY

## CHARACTERS

LYSISTRATA (LIZZY), 58 years old, participated in the feminist movement of 1968. Her name means disband the army.

MEDEA, a woman scorned with much suffering with sheer human agony and pain.

NORA, refuses to continue playing the Doll's role as if in a dolls house.

IRENE, refuses abusive treatment as a slave of society.

AMIE, accepted an abnormal situation in her life and is confused by what is normal and what is abnormal.

MOLLY, happy and sad about her relationship as she is over-involved in immoral behavior.

JEWEL, a young woman fed up and filled with rage.

JAKE, a Pastor with a dark past

MIKE, abused his wife.

PAUL, a schoolteacher with an alcohol problem

DAVID, a drug abuser

RALPH, a big guy who think he is tough.

ALI, confused with self.

SINGERS, OTHERS, off stage voices

# ACT I

## SCENE 1

Today, Middle-Class Americans are becoming displaced and do not know what to do with their lives. We spent time observing them as they battle with shame, disease, and self-destructiveness.

**SETTING:** Downtown Women's Shelter, it is near 12 Midnight. It is cold as the fall winds give way to the incoming frigid winter as Friday night gives way to the darkest hour of Saturday. The lighting is soft with dark shadows within the scene as the scene begins to play itself out. It appears that someone is in the space. Smooth jazz music is playing softly in the background. It is John Coltrane's Love Supreme playing from a radio as lights slowly fades in revealing a waiting room with crude type wooden chairs. There is a wooden table, where people could sit around to talk, play cards, or have counseling. A coffee urn heard brewing in the background. Lysistrata (also known as Lizzy) is standing by a frosty windowpane, holding a cup of coffee, in her hands. Lizzy's family has old money going back to the antebellum days in the South. She stands on the principle of projecting women into history alongside the dominant white males of European extraction. She is dressed in regular earthy type clothing, with a sweater over her shoulders, its arms tied around her chest. She appears as if she is waging war within herself over how far and how much she has gained in her battle for women liberation. We hear her soliloquy.

LIZZY: I am tired and angry of being a woman with some subliminal perceptive expectation of men to be a normal woman. I wish I could go back to the 1960s and pick up with the feminist movement calling for women liberation. Liberation... liberation... what is liberation? My fight and struggles are over. There is confusion between sex, gender, and transsexual. It seems anyone want to be a woman or a man. I do not have any children. My life is unfulfilled. I do not know where to go or what to do anymore. Most of my friends are married and have children. I am too far gone to turn around now. I am ashamed to go on Welfare. What if my friends see me? What will they say? But I do not have anywhere to go... to live ... to call Home ... I am Homeless ... I need health care ... I am a shame to ask for Medicaid ... What do I do? (She begins to cry, to herself)

JAKE: (*A man appears mopping the floor. He is listening. He is watching. He stares as Lizzy is crying. Then he speaks.*) Lizzy, what are you thinking about? You troubled about something.

LIZZY: One thing I do not need is some jack legged want to be preacher trying to tell me what I need to do or how I should think, I am not in the mood for any of your speeches. What are you doing here? You don't belong here. This is a Shelter for Women, It is not for has been men.

JAKE: I work here. I clean up around here. Besides I just wanted to help, We all need some kind of help. Why take me ... (*Door opens, we hear the roaring of cold wind*).

MEDEA: (*A woman runs into the scene from the outside moaning and crying. She is hysterical and babbling about her three babies ...*) I watched the icy waters move my babies ... three of them across the raging waves. The Moon Light spread a Satin Glow, I can still see their little dark eyes staring into my eyes as through any minute they would be gone. Then the Moon Glow was gone.

I stood petrified ... as the cold, dark water sucked ... each baby ... into its watery womb. *(She screams, then with anger)* I should have gotten rid of him! *(Now with a deep pain)Why did I... throw them ... over the bridge? Into the water! (As if to herself)* Why didn't I jump in? *(Lizzy and Jake stands looking as if shocked by what they overheard)*.

LIZZY: What are you saying? I know you are saying what I am thinking? What babies? You said ... Three babies? Jump in ... where? *(She thinks)* Thrown in? You got help me out here! *(Lizzy is about to lose it)* Tell me ... what are you talking about?

JAKE: Wait a minute! Wait a minute, let me handle this! Here *(Jake tenderly leads Medea to a chair, at the table)* sit here ... Lizzy get her a cup of coffee. *(Jake pulls up a chair, Lizzy brings the coffee)* Now, tell me, slowly ... tells us ... what happened?

MEDEA: She takes a sip of coffee, cups the coffee cup in her hands, looks into it as she place the cup gently on the table, staring into it) It is his fault... *(She reflects on what her husband did to her)* He started it ... *(She relives a tender moment)* ... He told me he loved me ...and that there would not be another in his life. *(And with a serious, deadly smile)* I believed him. *(And as if coming out of a dream)*... Then he went to prison. *(She breaks down and cries)* I waited for him. I visited him. I believed in him. *(Continues to cry as if she is looking him in the face, speaking to him)*. You should not have gone out ... when I needed you at home ... with our first child. However, you had to go be with your boys. *(Vindictively)* You see your boys got you into trouble with the law.

JAKE: What?

LIZZY: She is not talking to you ... just listen!

MEDEA: You write and tell me about your best friend ... you

call him your Cellmate ... Your Cellmate ... You even talked about him ... like he was your wife.

LIZZY: Oh no (*as she grasp*) this is painful ... I think I know where this is going.

MEDEA: Then you come home and the first thing you want to do with me is to have nasty sex. I can't stand you for making me perform that act with you. That is indecent and immoral ... and unclean. Then one night ... (*She gathers herself together*) you YELLED his name in frenzy. How...How...How could you have done this to me? You betrayed me and used me as a JAIL MATE! ... Me ... who ... was faithful to you. You violated my trust and my love for you. And now I hate you ... I hate you...you destroyed all that would remind me of you (*She shivers as if she is about to lose it*).

JAKE: Okay! Okay ... (*He compose himself*) Now tell us ... What about your babies? What did you say happen to them? (*In a quiet voice*) Where are they now?

MEDEA: (To the top of her voice) Where do you think they are? They are in HEAVEN! (She looks into Jake's eyes) I killed them! (*Silence prevails, the door opens and a cute little doll enters onto the stage ... We still hear a roar of heavy wind ... She is Nora. She comes from a well-to-do family*)

NORA: Jesus sent me! Sinners Repent! For the last days are at hand! Sinners, repent, repent, repent! The Lord sent me to turn you heathens from your wicked ways and to REPENT!

MEDEA: Oh Sister, HELP ME! I did something awful. I took life from my body! I killed my babies. (*She cries*) Now, I don't want to live. (*Hysterical*) Where are my babies? Where are their souls? They were swallowed up in the BELLY of the ocean. (*Nora stage crosses to Medea*)

NORA: (*With compassion*) Oh, my poor child. I can help you. Jake, get me a cup of black coffee. No, on second thought get me a drink. First, I need a drink. You got a drink. Anybody here got a drink. (Nervously) I NEED A DRINK!

JAKE: Nora Stop it! (Medea is sobbing and shaking) Can't you see this woman needs help... REAL HELP! You can't do anything for her. (*To himself*) I doubt if anyone can help her now.

NORA: (Tipsy) I don't think you all know who I am. I am a doctor.

LIZZY: You are not a doctor. You got a Ph.D. from Harvard. But, where has that got you? A DRUNK! You are nothing but a DRUNK. You come in here talking about repent. You are the one that need to repent. Save yourself! If you need to save someone save yourself.

NORA: You ... you call me a drunk. You don't even know who you are. You are nothing but a has-been feminist. You need a man; that's what you need. But you are afraid you can't get a man. Because you old, you too old to get a man. Besides, who would want you anyway?

JAKE: You know I can't stay here any longer. You are right Lizzy. I should not be here. This is a Shelter for woman. I need to get me another job. This is not working for me. You women are dealing with some serious issues. I took this job to forget about my problems. But me being here makes it unbearable for me to deal with my issues. I can't take it any longer.

MEDEA: (*Jake starts to leave this place*) You people are crazy! I came in here because of what I did. I had nowhere else to go. You all can't help me. You can't help yourselves. You all are sick. It is the BLIND LEADING THE BLIND.

---

NORA: BIRDS OF A FEATHER FLOCK TOGETHER, That's what the Elders say.

JAKE: Y'all need help. (*Jake places the mop against the wall and starts to leave*).

EVERYBODY: Wait! (*Jake stop as lights fades out*).


## ACT I

## SCENE 2

IRENE: (*Door open, Wind roars, sound of door slams shut, lights fades up revealing Irene standing there*) What's all the screaming about? I could hear noise coming from here a block away. Jake! Get me a cup of coffee! No cream! Lots of sugar! Be quick about! Alright Ladies, what's going on? What have I missed? Lizzy, Nora who is this? Someone else needs shelter here? (*She is looking at Medea*).

LIZZY: Yes, this is Medea. We just met her tonight. (*Looking at Medea*) This is Irene. Irene is a regular around. Nothing is ever right for Irene. She thinks, no, she believes the world owe her something.

NORA: Maybe it does! Heck, the world owes us all something. We give our lives to please man in his world. What do we get for it? Abuse! Violent Behavior! And no respect, yet he want to have a baby to prove he is a man. What brings you in out of the cold, Irene?

IRENE: Society! Economics! Politic! Governments! Young people are tearing down establishments. Women and Children and dying of hunger, thirst, and diseases and nobody is speaking up in their behalf. Society is going to the dogs!

LIZZY: You are a little too late for that; society has gone to the dogs. So why is it a problem for you? You can't do anything about.

IRENE: You are exactly right! That makes us slaves ... not being able to do anything about it. Society is a fake. Men changing into women because they do not want to be a man with responsibilities ... Women are changing into men to get back at the men for changing into woman. Other men are known as Down Low Men because they can go both ways being with a woman and being with a man. Plus there are Down Low Women going both ways. Then there are men and women child Predators abusing our children. Presidents, Congress, and Senators are leading society into Hell with deceptions and lies. Politicians are predators misleading their voters. I do not wish to be a part of this society. I wish to be alone. But I can't. I do not know what to do or where to go?

LIZZY: Join me Irene! Irene we just may be the answer to my needs. I need to get back in the fight. Join me in my fight for women liberation. (*Lizzy raises her fist*) Join me for Freedom! Freedom for women! Freedom for all women! Freedom can be for you Irene.

IRENE: What do you know about Freedom? You have been to the top. You know what it's like to have first-class citizenship. You had people arrested because you had enough money to have whoever you want arrested. You who slipped in and out of society at will. You can be a republican, democrat, independent. You can be a capitalist, communist, imperialist, or socialist, or nothing at all. But look at you now down in the slumps like the rest of us. Tell me what do you know about Freedom?

NORA: That is not fair, Irene! We all have been beaten down. We do not need to beat down each other. We all are in the same boat. Lizzy is just trying to recover and she wants to help you overcome your circumstances and situations. Let us face it! Lizzy got more experience in women issues. She just fell on hard times like the rest of us.

IRENE: Poor little Nora the middle-class Nora still chirping like a bird in a cage. Nora left her husband and children. You dolled yourself up every day to meet your husband at the front door looking like the little bird he first met. He had you in a bird cage to tweet for him. Nora, what happened when you tried to help him? He verbally abused you ... and you got your feelings hurt. You could no longer trust him ....believe in him. He betrayed you. Nora who lost herself in a whiskey bottle ... dedicates her life to John Barley Corn. What you and Lizzy need to do is to stay out of my business. You do not know me. You think you do but you don't!

JAKE: Yeah! I go along with that! You people think you know me but you don't. You know I drink a little too much, but you do not know why. You do not know who I am. You do not know my past or where I come from. I hang around here because you women give me strength. I see you come in and out of here with your problems about men, women, or with yourselves. But I come to the conclusion that you women need help. You are confused about yourselves, who you are, or where you come from. But, you do not do anything but...talks...about it. DO SOMETHING...MAKE A DIFFERENCE IN YOUR LIVES! (*Lights fade*).

# ACT I

## SCENE 3

*(Scene opens with everybody sitting and staring still...suddenly the door open a woman enters sobbing.)*

AMIE: *(Babbling to herself)* Oh! I am glad I am home ... now where did I leave my scarf. Children come bring mommy her scarf. I need my scarf. I have to have my scarf. Where did I put my scarf? *(Everybody focuses their attention onto Amie).*

LIZZY: Who are...? *(Lizzy is cut off my Jake).*

JAKE: *(A stage whisper)* Lizzy, let her be!

AMIE: *(Moving around as if she is in her house, tidying up)* I refused to be his sex object anymore. I refuse to be anybody's sex object anymore. But how will I live, all I know is to be cute and smile to get attention to attract a man, any man to get a job, just so I can live. *(Sitting)* But all I have done is to create a reality world that has placed a barrier against my vision to see ... What is real? Keeping it real? Being real is a delusion to keep me from being myself. I cannot live in this illusionary world thinking it is normal when it is abnormal, but I lived in an abnormal world so long that I think it is normal. Especially when I need something then I pretend to be normal in an abnormal life, in this world, to get it.

LIZZY: *(Whispering)* I cannot stand by and listen to this any longer. Who do you think you are sister? Coming in here with all that philosophy about what is or is not real.

AMIE: Do you live here too? I did not know anybody lived here but me. You are welcome to come into my world and talk with me, if you want too.

LIZZY: (*Looking around at the others*) You are sick. You need help!

JAKE: Is it not why we are here? We all need help. I told you to let her be. But no, you think you can recruit another for your movement to overthrown this world. You have to tear it down and remake a new world with you in it, to do that. (*A gush a wind blows the door open as Molly enters laughing and sobbing at the same time*) What now!

MOLLY: (*Wiping herself off*) That is nasty! That is nasty! I cannot stand to live here anymore. I must go live on an Island ... any Island ... anywhere but here. Is Irene here?

IRENE: (*Stage crossing toward Molly*) I am here, Molly. You still are having problems at home.

MOLLY: Yeah! Now he is smoking Meth and he wants me to fantasize with him. He placed a pole in the bedroom and he wants me in all kinds of position. He pours waste on my body. He makes me stand up naked in the bathroom and pour waste on me. Then he beats me for letting him abuse my body, by brain, and my spirit. He has broken me. I think about escaping and I am supposed to be a free woman in a free society. Irene, I need help!

JAKE: That is why I murdered my wife. (*Everyone stops short of whatever they were doing and stare at Jake*) Oh, they say it was self-defense, but it was murder. She wanted to change me ... you know ... make me over. So, eventually, I changed becoming what she thought I should be. Then she began to hate me for what I became. She said I was not the man she married ... that I was a stranger ... that she did not know me anymore. She began to hate herself. She began to hate me. One day I came home and she was baking a turkey. I walked up to her to hug her. She turned around and she carved me like I was the turkey. She drew blood. She had a crazed look in her eyes. I saw a kitchen knife on the counter. I picked it up. She came toward me with the knife. I panicked and I stuck her in her chest. She died of that one blow from the kitchen knife. I spend all this time by trying to help other woman to make up for killing my wife. But it is no use; I cannot help any of you.

MEDEA: My babies are dead! I killed them. Help me now! I need help. I am losing it. I am going mad. (*She Babbles*)

ALL: Help us all!

JAKE: (*Jake leaves the stage.*)

## ACT II

**SETTING:** Everyone is sitting as if in a daze. Every once in a while there is heard a sigh and a moan. Coltrane is heard in the background. It is silent now. Moments later, we can hear the wind blowing and the sound of a train passing through the shelter. The women move closer to each other as if to pray to the God of their understanding. The door opens as if the wind has blown it open. The women turn and look toward the open door. After a moment, a young woman slowly enters. She's in shock; finger and thumb clinches her lips; her body twitches; her eyes piercing, and her head jerks. She appears as if she had been in a rage. She mumbles. She crosses downstage center and stand with eyes fixed into space.

JEWEL: Enough ... enough ... enough ... I had enough ... enough ... enough ... fed up! Over and over and over ... I have taken the pain ... the agony ... the disrespect... the abuse ... I refuse to take no more ... enough ... enough ... I had enough!

WOMEN: (*Women slowly stage cross, hovering around Jewel. Medea is right stage of Jewel and Molly is left stage of Jewel).*

IRENE: What is she saying? What is she really saying?

AMIE: She said she is fed up and she had enough. You know she is through dealing with whatever she was dealing with.

NORA: It must be about a man! It is always about a man!

JEWEL: *(Jewel screams jumping up and down! She digs into her hair, with her finger tips, eyes popping out, her head moving from side to side, hysterical, emotional, and fill with fear).* Awwwwwwwwwww ... it will not go away ... awwwwwwwwwwwww.
LIZZY: Sister, what's the matter? What is wrong with you? What do we do?

MOLLY: What happen? Sugar ... did someone do something wrong too you?

JEWEL: *(Standing as a soldier)* I am a soldier! I can go through anything ... whatever for my country.

AMIE: What do you mean ... honey? You been in the military?

JEWEL: I am a student!

MOLLY: Okay, what kind of student?

JEWEL: I just completed my freshman year in college! He was a senior! He should have known better!

NORA: What are you talking about?

JEWEL: (Looking at the women to her left and to her right, and then raises her left fingers to her fore head) We were living together! He was...

IRENE: Was? Were? (*Irene searches her thoughts*) What did you do?

JEWEL: I don't know where to begin? (*As she questions her mind fill with thoughts of fear and rage at the same time*).

MEDEA: Come! Sit down with us, at the table. Someone get a cup of coffee! (*The women stage crosses toward and gather around the table*).

JEWEL: (*Jewel look into the eyes of each women*) All of you have hurt in your eyes! (*She sits center at the table*).

LIZZY: Please take this cup of coffee, it is black. Do you want cream and sugar?

JEWEL: (*Taking the cup of black coffee*) No ... (*Looking around at the women*) ... thank you.

IRENE: Were you in the military?

JEWEL: (*Sipping coffee*) Yes!

IRENE: (*Trying not to pry ... too much ... being careful not to push Jewel into talking*) Did you serve in Iraq?

JEWEL: Yes (*as she begin to stare off as though she could see herself in uniform in Iraq*).

NORA: Did you see action? While ... 'you ... were ... there.

JEWEL: Yes (*Jewel clinches the coffee cup as she bring it up to her forehead ... she slowly lowers the cup to the table*) I saw dead women and babies ... I saw bodies on top of bodies ... I saw pools of blood ... it made me sick to my stomach.

AMIE: You don't have to talk about it...if you don't want too.

JEWEL: (*Searching Amie's eyes*) I seen a troop put a gun to his head and pulled... the trigger ... in rage. I don't think he knew what he was doing. He reacted! It frightened me. I was scared!

MOLLY: Wow! (*Molly cannot conceive of what it would like for her in that situation*) What did you do?

JEWEL: I cried ... but I kept moving. Later, we went out on patrol... searching for the enemy. I thought to myself ... I am seventeen going on eighteen ... I could be home going to school preparing for a career and a family ... and here I am looking to kill or be killed ... I don't know how I made eighteen months of hell!

MEDEA: How old are you now?

JEWEL: Twenty-one!

LIZZY: Earlier, you said, you were "fed up." What did you mean by that?

JEWEL: What do you think I meant?

LYSISTRATA: Well, when I say I am fed up ... I am fed up with men. I am fed up with society. I am fed up with who I am. I am fed up with life. I am fed up with...

MEDEA: (*Stopping Lizzy*) Nobody is talking about...Lizzy ... we are all fed up with something ... What is your name ... honey?

JEWEL: Jewel

MEDEA: Jewel... you also said you had enough ... enough of what?

JEWEL: (*Jewel stands up hysterically*) Enough of men putting their hands on my body...

NORA: Who put their hands on your body ... Jewel?

AMIE: Were you raped?

JEWEL: (*Crying hysterically*) I joined the military to serve my country, to build a career for myself and eventually a family, and to go to college ... not to be raped by my follow comrades...

IRENE: Oh no...

MOLLY: Not the troops you served with...

AMIE: That's awful...

NORA: I cannot believe it. ..

MEDEA: They did something like that to you...

LIZZY: That hurts ... How did it happen?

JEWEL: (*Jewel begins to relive her experience*) We had returned to Post after running into an IED on the road. We lost lives and suffered much injury. The men were in rage and feeling a sense of being let down. I headed straight for the John which was located off to the side of the barracks. I was preparing to enter the John to relieve myself when an arm appeared around my neck, pulling me to the back side of the John. As I struggled to free myself, another soldier grabbed me around my legs (*Jewel is breathing heavily as she tells her story*) and started taking my trousers down. Someone hit me in the face ... hard ... I blinked ... As I regained my sight I saw one soldier holding my arms, another was holding my legs, and one soldier was on top of me ... I was humiliated ... (*sobbing with anger*) ... they took turns ... I wanted to die.

MOLLY: My God, I didn't know that these things were happening with our men and women in uniform ... fighting for our country ... fighting for us ... Oh God!

AMIE: Jewel, I hope you do not take this lying down ... giving up ... living into an illusionary world ... and by the way ... did you report this ... too anyone.

JEWEL: (*Very stern*) Yes ... I did!!

LIZZY: Ok! So justice was done ... RIGHT? I mean they got what they deserved ... didn't they? What happened, Jewel?

JEWEL: There was not even a Court-Martial. Nothing happened!

NORA: Well, how long have you been back from the War!

JEWEL: One year...

IRENE: Wait a minute! Just one minute! You came in here earlier looking like you were crazed out of your mind. You cannot tell me you have been laying up somewhere thinking about what happened to you in Iraq ... What happened that brought you in here?

AMIE: Yeah ... that's right... what brought you in here, tonight!

JEWEL: I killed my boyfriend.

MOLLY: Say what! You did what?

JEWEL: I killed my boyfriend!

MEDEA: Let's get this straight... you came in here talking about being abused while serving in the military ... and now you are telling us you came in here tonight because you killed your boyfriend ... you got some explaining to do ... Sister!

JEWEL: I said I was fed up and I had enough! I did not want to be abused again... by another man. So I killed him.

LIZZY: What did this man do to you that made you kill him?

JEWEL: We had an argument. .. his voice was loud ... my head swelled...I heard voices...I was back in uniform...he sound hysteria...He left the apartment...I reached for the kitchen knife...if he comes back I will kill him ... I looked out the window...He was coming back...I stood in the doorway...I watched him walk up the stairs ... as he reached the landing...he faced me ... I struck him in the neck with the knife ... he reached for his neck...I struck him in the jugular vein...blood poured out...I watched him trying to hold back the blood pouring out of him...he staggered and fell dead ...I started walking out into the night...it started to rain. The rain washed the blood from my hand...the knife slipped out from my hand and fell to the ground ...it began to thunder then lightening...I saw the sign saying "Shelter" and I came in here...

WOMEN: (*Responding with shock!*)

MOLLY: When you came in here you said he was a senior and that you are a freshman. This man you killed ... was he the senior you started to talk about?

JEWEL: Yes...

AMIE: Jewel, this happened just before you came in here ... RIGHT?

JEWEL: Yes it did.

IRENE: Then...the police are looking for you.

JEWEL: I am sure of it. (*Sirens are heard from afar, then closer and louder, cars come to a screeching halt, as sirens continue*)

POLICE NEGOTIATOR: (*Off stage voice*) Jewel Robinson...we know you are in there...come out with your hands in the air.

LIZZY: They know she is in here. How do they know that?

IRENE: Because somebody saw her and told them she is in here, how do you think the police know... because somebody tells them...that's how?

JEWEL: What do I do? I am so confused. I am beginning to hear voices ... telling me to fight my way out of here...I need help!

MOLLY: Jewel, that's why we are here...we need help.

AMIE: Let's stand behind Jewel; she has been through a lot. Who can we call?

MEDEA: Let's pray about it first!

LIZZY: You can count me out! I did not come here to go to church. Prayer never done anything for me...besides, I don't believe in a God...

MEDEA: Let's join hands!

POLICE NEGOTIATOR: I said to come out with your hands up, you have five minutes and we are coming in.

MEDEA: Who's Father (*The women repeat the Lord's Prayer, except Lizzy who stand looking at the women in prayer*).

WOMEN: Amen!

LIZZY: Amen…

AMIE: You said you didn't pray!

LIZZY: Shut up!

IRENE: Lizzy! Tell them she's coming out…

LIZZY: (*Stage cross toward door, opens it and shout*) She is coming out… (*Lizzy looks around at Jewel*) with her hands up!

IRENE: Let's walk with her! (*The women gather around Jewel and stage cross toward the door. Lights slowly fade as Police red lights intensify, and then the stage turns to dark*).

POLICE VOICE: (*Stage is dark*) Raise your hands higher!


# ACT III

## SCENE 1

**SETTING:** Men's Group meeting in a Men's Shelter, Mike, Paul, David, Ralph, Jake, and Ali are in a discussion concerning issues they feel they have to face each day as they live and breathe. There is a table, big and roomy enough for the men to spread out as will. There is a coffee pot or urn, where the men periodically go for coffee, They are center stage with bright over head lights down upon them as the light leaks into the dark stages up, right, and left, Jake is talking as the scene opens,

The men are curious as to what Jake is telling them. Some men agree with him and some men do not agree with.

JAKE: I figured by working in the Women's Shelter I would try to help women with their issues since I failed my marriage by ending it with her death. By serving time, society says I've paid my debt for the crime. Yet, I know deep down inside of me that I could've walked away when I saw she was suffering from stinking thinking, You know the kind of thinking that get you into trouble,

RALPH: (*A big guy who think he is tough but hides fears of being found out*) You just hit something in me with that stinking thinking. I heard someone in a 12 Step program talking about Stinking Thinking. How does that work?

MIKE: (*Abused his wife*) I am not sure but I think it goes something like this. You find yourselves thinking on something...could be anything...maybe you thinking about that girl you lost, 'cause usually it is about another person...someone you think you care about...but really you care only about yourself...you be tripping about when you cheated on that girl you lost...as you see yourself playing around...after a while you start thinking that maybe she is playing around and was cheating on you...too. You slowly forget that you started out thinking about that girl you had fun with...yeah at first...you were thinking about who you were playing around with. That was before you took that mental drift into a scene playing out in your mind about the girl you lost....After a while, you don't see yourself playing the field anymore...you just see her playing around...on you ... (*Looking at Ralph*)...playing around. Now your feelings hurt...

PAUL: (*A schoolteacher with an alcohol problem*) I get it! That's when stinking thinking begins...when your feelings get involve and you start talking all about how she must have been slipping

100

around on you...you forget you were the one slipping around on her...but now you done rationalized your guilt by placing all the blame on her...Cause you out the picture now...it is just her and him or him and her playing around...on you. You start seeing images of her playing around in your head ... you get nervous ... you breathing hard...you can almost reach out and grab her throat...you want to hurt her...because you are now hurt ... you looking for the payback...you see them in your mind...you can hear them...talking about you...you get mad...your stinking thinking think it is real...you want to do something...you want to catch them in the act...you see yourself catching them in the act You are hurt and emotional...you feel you need something...some courage...You start thinking about getting high...a shot of liquor...

DAVID: (*A Drug Abuser*) Or a shot of Dope ... Yeah, a shot of liquor, a shot of smoke, a shot of this and a shot of that ... a shot is still nothing more than a shot. So you take a shot of dope ... now you really feeling like you in charge...in charge with false pride... inflated ego...paranoid...now you are crazy... insane... you want to react...react to your stinking thinking. Yeah, you want to give her a piece of your mind... your crazy mind tell you where she is...your mind is filled with patterns and behaviors of your time spent with her...you convinced yourself that she is with the other guy...the guy your stinking thinking made up in your crazed mind...Yeah, you done caught her in act with this imaginary guy...But first you need a shot of that John Barley Corn, that White Girl, or that Bad Boy, or that Crack with that glass dick in your mouth...so you think you need to have that false courage...But you start feeling pity for yourself... Yeah that self-pity...making you believe you are the victim...when you are the perpetrator.

ALI: (Ali is confused with self) You who have so little faith...John Barley Corn...False Pride...Self-Pity...You think you know everything...but you don't know anything...you think you have all the answers. You allow yourselves to get caught up into stinking thinking. Like you are playing God or something like that, you were the playwright, the actor, and the director of your little...stinking...thinking...world. You people lost...I am not like you! (*Pride*) Yeah, take me for instant, I don't eat pork. I don't eat a lot of things. I don't let poison enter my body, my soul, or my brain. I keep myself clean at all times. I am not dirty like the rest of you all. You HEARD ME! I am not like YOU!

MIKE: Okay Ali, you are better than the rest of us. You just here cause you just stopped by to see how the rest of us are living, RIGHT! But, I just need to know one thing...WHY ARE YOU HERE...in this... (*Looks around*)...in this Men's Shelter. I mean...you don't seem to have a problem...or do you? Or is it that you don't have anywhere else to go...DO YOU?

JAKE: Whoa! Lighten up, Mike. Maybe, Ali just got of jail or from some other institution...you know (*takes a finger and motion a swirl around his head*) and don't have nowhere else to go. But what difference does it make...we are all here...so tell me what are we going to do to take our rightful place in society. We all have burnt bridges. We destroyed our relationships. Nobody wants us around anymore. We are HOMELESS and this here is our Shelter. We have nowhere else to go ... BUT UP! (*Points up*).

RALPH: I don't know! I keep thinking about my brother. He was strung out on drugs. He was caught in that stinking thinking. He robbed from his family, stole from his friends. Yeah, he even stole money out of the church offering plate during morning services. He ended up in a mental hospital...The Veterans Affairs Medical Center for Mental Disease from alcohol and drugs. There he was exposed to a 12-Step program. He was given a sponsor and together they worked a recovery program. That was twenty years ago, today, taking it one day at a time miracles have worked in his life. If you saw him today you would not know he was that same fellow. Anyway, I don't know what will work for me...I just don't know...

PAUL: You don't know what? You talked about your brother and I can see how you sharing that can help some of us. But, that is your brother. What's up with you? What are you talking about? You started off talking about "I don't know?" What don't you know?

ALI: Man, can't you see he is afraid! Paul...Ralph is hiding something. He is hiding from himself. I know when someone is hiding something. I...

MIKE: Ralph...what are you afraid of?

RALPH: Well! I...I...I have problems with who I am...

DAVID: What you mean? You have problems with who you are. Are you funny, man? Or you just don't know who you are.

RALPH: I know who I am...I just...don't know... how... to...get...along...with...

PAUL: You don't know how to get along with what?

RALPH: With…with…woman, I don't know how to relate to women.

JAKE: Well, if that's the case ... nobody knows how to get along with women (*everyone smiles*).

ALI: You know, I believe we all suffer from Post-Traumatic Stress Disorders brought on us by the harsh treatment our forefathers endured from a racist, slave society that crippled our bodies and diseased our brains where today we cannot think properly and we are suffering from all kinds of diseases that our forefather and foremothers did not have before they were chained down into hot, sweltering ship beds laden with filthy urine and feces...humiliating our people. I have dreams of dry bones reaching out to me...man that is scary.

JAKE: That is depressing, Ali. Leroi Jones described it just like that in his play "Slave Ship." Everybody got to read that play. When I saw the play in Newark, New Jersey, Leroi locked the theatre doors; we found ourselves in complete darkness. In the next instance, there were sounds of rattling chains, then suffocating smells; it was like smells of an outhouse, then sounds of moans. The audience was uncomfortable. Leroi had white audiences seated in the side rows, while Black audience sat in the middle rows. Some of the white audience patrons got up to leave and could not get out the doors because they were locked. The white audience patrons yelled "let us out of here." The theater lights slowly faded in as stage sounds got louder from moans to screams of suffering pain. Then there were the screams of the white audience patrons and the screams of suffering slaves chained on tiers which appeared to be in the hull of a "Slave Ship." Wow, Ali what you said brought all those images back to me. Is it that we all suffer from Post-Traumatic Stress/Slave Disorders brought on by that harrowing experience our ancestors suffered and endured that continues to plague us? It is an "Amazing Grace." For the music of that song was the heartbeats and moans of our people crossing over...crossing over to injustice.

ALI: Yes, that is what it is! I am hurt and I am filled with anger. Injustice has been done to my people ... His-story has hidden Our-story from us ... Like the Gullah Wars...between 1739-185...which drove presidents of these United States up the wall. It was the Battle of the Gullah Warriors that demanded our Emancipation, not Abe Lincoln or the Civil War...That was just to cover up their failure to subdue us...even after they killed our mothers, daughters, sisters, brothers, and so forth. Injustice done to our people and injustice has been done to me. I spent time in the military. I was a good kid before I joined. I was glorifying the notion of serving my country...a country that just wanted to use me up and spit me out. I was all connected with my family, classmates, community, and the girl I knew I would spend the rest of my life with. I got disconnected while l was in the military. I didn't know who I was anymore. I didn't know who I had become neither. I could not fit in when I returned home. Everybody said I had changed. They said they didn't know how to talk to me. I felt alone. I eventually wandered away from everybody...everybody I loved. So I became numb. I got no feelings. I don't want to hurt, or be hurt no more.

PAUL: That is real. I can't face myself because I have not been real with myself and so I have not been real with anybody else...I mean nobody else. Yeah man, that was real... I always said, "I am hurting nobody but myself...but that is not true." By hurting myself, I hurt all those around me, especially those who loved me...Wow...that hurts. Feelings, feelings, feelings and more feelings...my head hurts from feelings.

MIKE: Yeah, I know about feelings. I know all about feelings...men, women, and children dying from feelings. Feelings got them dying from HIV/AIDS. Shucks! I know alcoholics and drug addicts strung out due to feelings, and what about brothers and sisters in prison and on death row behind feelings. Yeah! I know all about feelings. Feelings are what got me here...down and out... and that hurts.

RALPH: I hear you! Feelings are associated with "Like" (*uses fingers to mimic quotes*) you know...being concerned with whether somebody likes you or not. I made the mistake looking for someone to like me, instead of whether or not they were doing RIGHT by me. See, like...is for little children...they either like this or like that or they don't like this or like that. As a man, I need to know whether you doing right by me or not.

JAKE: I never thought about it like that before. I thought you were supposed to make people like you.

DAVID: Yeah, I got caught up in that word, too.

JAKE: What word?

DAVID: THOUGHT! I thought she was supposed to love me. I thought I was going to finish college. I thought I was going to get that job I knew was mine. I thought and I thought but none of those things happened. I started feeling sorry for myself. Yeah, I said it. FEELING! I was at a party drowning in a glass of beer when a friend of mine said I look down and out and that he knew what could pick me up. I said what the hell. Man, what you got. We walked into the men's room. We went into a stall. He pulled out his works and heated a spoon of Boy. It was only a skin pop and I was off to the races. You see I thought about things that never happened and ended up giving away everything I had.

JAKE: So, you still feeling sorry for yourself. It sounds to me that we are all here because you are feeling sorry for ourselves. Talking about poor me... poor me...yeah, pour me another drink. Damn!

ALI: Wow! I have been carrying around inside of me a hold lot of hurt and pain. I didn't want to talk about it because I thought I was unique and that no other man suffered the way I did ... until now.

MIKE: Yeah! I have been carrying around a hold lot of guilt and shame that eats through me. My wife was not cheating on me. I was cheating on her. I became afraid that she would find out and that I would lose her. So, I started thinking maybe she is cheating on me too. After a while of thinking on her cheating me, my feelings got involved. I downed a couple shots of liquor to calm my nerves. Instead of my nerves being calmed, the shots of liquor gave me false courage to face her. I accused her of cheating on me. She denied it. She accused me of lying on her. One thing led to the next and before I knew it I had swung on her. I could have stopped but my pride would not let stop, so I continued to pound on her until I had enough. Then, I immediately became sorry for what I allowed myself to do to her. Guilt set in and I became ashamed of myself. I loved her and yet I hated her all at the same time.

PAUL: You loved her, but you hated yourself.

MIKE: Yeah, I guess so. Thanks fellows, I had all that and more locked down in me. It is like a weigh lifted off of me.

JAKE: More shall be revealed, Mike, as soon as possible, you need to made amends to her for what you did and why you did it.

MIKE: I am ashamed to do so.

DAVID: That is your reason for making amends, she may or may not accept your amends, but at least you would be willing to make amends and restitution if any are due. Making amends is for you and maybe for her too, especially when it brings no injuries.

ALI: You willing to make amends to her.

MIKE: Yes, I am willing to make amends to her. (*Takes in a deep breath and let it out*).

RALPH: (*Ralph speaks after there is a moment of silence*) I saw my mother abused by my step-father. Daddy died when I was nine years old. Mom, she did her best to raise us. She worked two jobs. I being the oldest wanted to be the man of the house but momma said, "go to school, get an education, and be somebody." My little brother was interested in playing with his games but he always heard momma and me talking. My sister was grown by the time Momma brought home this man. She told my brother and me to call him Father. I know now I rebelled. I said he is not my Father...my Father is dead...and I will not call him Father. The old man put up with it for a while. Then he started yelling at my mother. I would break up their argument and threaten him that if he touched my mother, I would kill him. He started staying out later and later after work without coming home. Then the day came that he never returned to us again. Some nights I could hear my mother sobbing alone in her room. I don't know if she was sobbing for my dead father, the step-father who left, or for me. Momma was never the same. I isolated myself from women after that. I guess I just didn't want to hurt another woman again.

DAVID: Where is your mother?

RALPH: She died a few years ago.

DAVID: Did you get a chance to talk about these things with her and to ask her how she felt?
RALPH: No, I didn't.

JAKE: Where is her grave?

RALPH: It's not that far away.

JAKE: Go to her graveside, bring some flowers, spend some time and talk with her. Tell her everything. Start from the time your Father died all the way up until now.
RALPH: I will.

PAUL: Oh Wow! I did some things I am not proud of. I left my family for another woman. What makes it so bad is that I worked with the other woman. I remember saying to my wife that there was nothing I would do to break up our happy home. It started one night when I came home from work. I was excited that I had been offered a position in the school system where I would earned more money. I wanted to celebrate with my wife. I know now I didn't take into consideration that her day was not like my day. She had a hard day with the children, but I didn't pay attention to her mood. I was so excited that I was just thinking about myself. I accused her not sharing with my success that it meant nothing to her that I had a raise. We argued and I felt like my feelings were hurt, so I grabbed my coat and run out of the house. I ran down to the corner bar and I ordered a double. I had a few. I recognized the woman coming toward me. I had seen her at the school I worked at. She walked up to me and smile. I was already tipsy so I offered her a drink. I watched her as she sat down on the bar stool. I felt a strong urge come over me and I imagined we were celebrating my success: I don't remember much after that until I woke up. I lift my eyelids open very slowly. I didn't know where I was. Then I heard someone speak. It was not my wife. It was the other woman. I never forgave myself for that. At first I accused my wife of not being to me like I thought she should be. That one act cost me my wife and my lovely children. Now I work just to keep me a bottle. I am sick and tired of being sick and tired.

JAKE: Paul, you can forgive yourself.

PAUL: I did not know that!

MEN: Now we know we can start making amends to forgive ourselves, first, for the injustice we brought upon ourselves and to our families.

JAKE: Then we can make amends to others whether they accept them or not, we made them. And men I found out from a man locked up in the VA Mental Hospital that I can love myself.

ALI: What you mean by that?

DAVID: I think I know what he mean...I did not love myself after I cheated on my wife and that is when I lost love for my wife and my children...ooooo that hurts! Now I know I can or at least learn to forgive and to love myself, and then perhaps I can love my family enough to go to them and ask their forgiveness. If I still have a family.

MIKE: Yeah, they remembered when you took up loving them drugs, chasing, and sucking on a stem, a pipe, a ... a ... glass dick!

RALPH: Mike, you don't have to be so hard on David.

DAVID: Wow, I just got an image of myself doing exactly that, Thanks, Ralph! But Mike is right. That is what I did. I have to face that fact and begin to change my behavior. But I need you guys to help me. I don't think I can do it by myself, Thanks Mike for being hardcore about it.

MIKE: That is an act of love...tough love...but David is making a point. Nobody knows me like you guys do...I mean we have opened up to each other, because we are men with issues who have tried to solved our problems by ourselves, because we didn't want someone...anyone to think something was wrong with us...which is was. I mean do I make sense.

ALI: You make a lot of sense Mike. When we walk away from this Shelter we are back to the races... anything goes. We need to have a gathering where we can discuss among ourselves how we are getting along and what is going on in our lives. What Mike is saying is that we identify with each other because we suffered from the same pain. Pain coming from an empty void in our lives, it didn't go away because we had not been honest with ourselves or with anybody else.

PAUL: I agree! We need to meet one, two, or three times a week. We need to set a time to meet. We need to have a place to meet at.

JAKE: I can arrange for us to meet here Tuesday, Thursday, and Friday nights at 7:00 p.m. until we find a place we can meet regularly.

MEN: That will work!

RALPH: What do we call our meeting? (*The men give it some thought*).

DAVID: How about Shelter from the Storms of Life?

MEN: (*Nods from heads in agreement*).

JAKE: Sounds good! We can always change it later if we want to. I like the idea of us forming a discussion group.

ALI: Jake, with due respect, I believe we would like to think of it as a Men Support Group. (*Men nod heads in agreement*).

JAKE: I like that better! We agree ... (*Jake extends his left fist out, each man one at a time extends his fist lining up with each extended fist until a circle is formed*).

MEN: WE AGREE! (*Lights fade until out as song "Never Could Have Made It" is played - Lyrics by Marvin L. Sapp and Matthew Richard Brownie, 2007*).

# ACT III

## SCENE 2

**SETTING:** Women Shelter. Women are sitting with cups of coffee in hands as music is heard in the background.

MEDEA: Jewel coming in here woke me up. I left the Mental Hospital without using my Meds or returning to aftercare treatment. But tonight, Jewel gave me a reason and a purpose to help myself by understanding, what happened to me and to get honest with myself.

NORA: Drinking liquor did not solve my problem it only added more fuel to the fire. Coming in here is like coming home. You know Amie made a point about coming in calling this home. Well, if coming in here telling my story of what is going on in my life helps me to get through one day at a time ... then this home.

IRENE: Nobody will listen to me anywhere else except in these rooms because we all can identify with each other because we share the PAIN. That empty void deep within us that aches and hurts us. Coming here and sharing our lives helps fill that void. Thanks to you all for being here for me.

AMIE: When I come here I am met with honesty. It is that honesty that helps me through my illusions and I am able to have a piece of saneness. I can go on a little bit further putting one foot in front of the other.

MOLLY: I need you women in my life. You have issues and so do I. Here we talk about them when we cannot talk to our blood relatives or to our so-called friends. I cannot, talk to my

---

Pastor or to the Deacons in my Church about my issues. I tried that and I was proportioned for it.

LIZZY: I have to make amends to you all. I have been waging liberation for all women from men. I have been building a movement only to find it was only in my head, while the women around me are trying to free themselves from themselves. I have not been listening to any of you...really. But now I hear you. We need to meet more often...on a regular basis.

NORA: Lizzy, are you saying we have issues but you don't?

LIZZY: No, I have issues...serious issues of denial.

WOMEN: We all do!

MEDEA: Okay, we meet here Tuesday, Thursday, and Saturday at 8:00 pm until we find a regular meeting place.

IRENE: Put the word out to all women that a Women Support Group is here and we take it One Day at a Time.

AMIE: Let's call it that, "One Day at a Time."

*(Lights fade to song. "We've Come This Far by Faith," Lyrics and music by Albert A. Goodson , 1956.)*

# THE BROTHERS by Publius Terentius Afer (Terence)

(195?-159 B.C.)

Publius Terentius Afer was the educated man's Plautus, a writer of six high comedies that made him the Philip Barry of his age. He was a devoted follower of Greek models of literary taste and polish, so that to know the plays of Terence is also to know the Greek New Comedy as written by its fourthcentury master, Menander; Julius Caesar admiringly called Terence a "half-Menander." With this successor to Plautus we come curiously close to the Augustan age of Roman refinement, which did not actually begin until about a century and a quarter after Terence's death. His dexterity in evolving a plot and his skill in shaping a character are accomplishments unapproached until his time and unequaled in Latin literature thereafter.

Terence was a native Carthaginian, the product of a Semitic civilization then dying out as a result of military conquest by Rome. Of either Negro or Berber extraction, he was brought to Rome as a slave in his youth but was educated in the household of a liberal senator and given his freedom. Handsome and refined, Terence was quickly received into the intellectual circle of the aristocracy and became a close friend of its leader, Scipio Africanus Minor. Influenced by his friends' fashionable taste for Greek learning and probably encouraged by the success of an older contemporary writer of high comedy, Caecilius Statius (219?-166? B.C.), also not a Roman, but a manumitted Gaul, Terence wrote like a Hellene for his Roman audiences.

Terence's first play, Andria, was produced in Rome in 166 B.C. He founded it on a comedy of the same title by Menander, and it appears to have received the approval of the influential Caecilius, to whom he is said to have read his manuscript.

Nevertheless, Terence encountered sharp opposition from a rival playwright and the latter's clique on the grounds that he was guilty of contaminatio--that is, of taking liberties with the Greek original by mixing its plot with details taken from other plays. He was also accused of receiving assistance from his cultivated friends. The same charges were made against all his later work, and the accusation of contaminatio irked him as much as the competition he faced from popular forms of entertainment side shows and rope-dancing interludes to which the Roman masses were more susceptible than to high comedy. Terence wrote prologues to his plays justifying his free treatment of the original Greek comedies and his fusing the plots of several of these. This was, indeed, the method of playwriting which he consistently employed, although he probably invented scenes and characterizations himself. In his prologues he also embodied a plea for critical standards and good taste, hoping to lift the public up to his level.

Productions were difficult for Terence to obtain; his plays were put on mainly with the help of highly situated friends and of the leading actor of his time, Ambivius Turpio, who staged 'them with music specially written by a certain Flaccus, the gifted slave of the aristocrat Claudius. Lacking the rowdy humor and ingenious versification of Plautus, and departing from his contagious "song-and-dance" routine, Terence could not command immense popularity although four of his plays won some favor and another, The Eunuch, became a popular success. But his urbanity marked a great advance in Roman playwriting. Ii, instead of following the direction in which he pointed, Rome returned to the farce comedies of Plautus with increased relish and turned, indeed, from ill Greek-inspired comedy (fabula palliata) to a new, robust national comedy of Roman scenes and costumes (fabula togata), Terence is nonetheless an important figure in the European drama. His were the only comedies that the medieval world was to find morally acceptable, and the Renaissance considered his plays the most refined models for high comedy.

Terence wrote pithy natural speech addressed to cultivated ears. Relying on characterization to a great degree--despite the frequent presence of coincidence in his standardized, less than plausible plots--he set the first example of high comedy from which playwrights could learn anything, once the Greek originals had vanished. Dispensing with prefatory plot summaries, employing suspense in plot construction, and substituting development by dialogue for the more customary narrative monologues, he exemplified a new technique. Even his use of conventional asides advanced dramaturgy, because his were true soliloquies conveying the characters' thoughts instead of crude declamations to the audience. In his own time, consequently, Terence stood with the literary vanguard.

The plays of Terence won him considerable social standing, and it is not improbable that friends presented him with some property. He appears to have left an estate along the Appian Way to a daughter, who later married a Roman senator. Possibly with a view to acquiring more Greek plays for adaptation, Terence took a journey to Greece in 159 B.C., and he was never seen again. The circumstances of his death are not known.

Romantic sentiment prevails in the first Terentian comedy, Andria, or The Woman of Andros, in which a young lover succeeds in marrying the supposed sister of a courtesan in spite of his father's objections. (Andria served as the basis of Richard Steele's sentimental comedy The Conscious Lovers, 1722, as well as of Thornton Wilder's novel, The Woman Andros). Terence's next play, The Self-Tormentor (163 B.C.), contains greater emphasis on characterization, although it too is a comedy of love and intrigue resolved by a discovery. It was followed in 161 B.C. by the author's most successful, because it is his most lively, work, The Eunuch, which, with Plautus' Miles Gloriosus, or The Braggart Soldier, provided the basis for the first fully realized pre-Shakespearean comedy, Nicholas Udall's Ralph Roister Doister. Although there is some salacious matter in the device of a young man posing as a eunuch in order to gain access into the house of the girl he intends to ravish, the effect of the writing is pleasant and exuberant. The play was certainly well suited to the occasion of the production, the feast in honor of Cybele, the Roman goddess of fertility. Phormio, produced at the Roman games in the same year, was almost as vivacious, largely as a result of the intrigues of the parasite Phormio, who is the most delightful stock character in classic comedy. It is, however, in the last play, Adelphi, or The Brothers, produced in 160 B.C., that the Terentian vein of high comedy runs most purely. Although it has the usual plot of sentimental attachments and misunderstandings, the action is resolved by logic of characterization rather than by conventional farcical tricks and coincidences. The substance of the writing, in fact, makes The Brothers the first extant "problem comedy" of European literature. The true subject is not the standardized romance but the question of what is the best policy to apply to youth-discipline or understanding tolerance. Two theories of education are contrasted by Terence, and the action demonstrates the validity of Terence's point of view, which favors tolerance. Among the later plays engendered by this work is Moliere's The School for Husbands. We cannot overestimate the influence of this first known stress on an intellectual approach in comedy of manners upon the Western theatre that later produced Moliere, Sheridan, Shaw, Barry, and Behrman. In spirit, The Brothers is hardly Roman at all; it is a late evocation of Greek humanism.

# Didascalia

The Brothers of Terence. Acted at the Funeral Games in honour of Lucius Aemilius Paulus which were given by Quintus Fabius Maximus and Publius Cornelius Africanus. The chief actors were Lucius Ambivius Turpio and Lucius Atilius Praenestinus. It was set to music by Flaccus, slave of Claudius, to the accompaniment of Tyrian flutes. It is from the Greek of Menander and is the poet's sixth play. It was presented during the consulship of Marcus Cornelius Cethegus and Lucius Anicius Gallus (160 B.C.).

## Summary

Since Demea has two sons, he permits his brother Micio to adopt Aeschinus but he him-self keeps Ctesipho. Demea was a harsh and strict fatherland when Ctesipho fell in love with a music girl his brother Aeschinus concealed it and took on himself the blame for the love affair; finally he took the music girl away from the pimp. Aeschinus had already seduced an impoverished Athenian girl and had promised to marry her. Demea upbraids him and is greatly vexed. Later, when the truth is revealed, Aeschinus marries the girl he has wronged and Ctesipho retains possession of the music girl.

## Prologue

When the poet found that his writings were likely to be attacked by malicious critics, and that his adversaries did all in their power to discredit the play we are now going to act, he resolved to give evidence regarding himself, and leave it to your judgment, whether what they reproach him with is worthy of praise or blame.

---

118

The Synapothnescontes is a comedy written by Diphilus. Plautus has rendered it into Latin, and called it Commorientes. In the Greek of Diphilus there is a youth, who, in the beginning of the play, takes a girl by force from a pimp. This Plautus has left untouched, and our poet has transferred it word for word into his Brothers, a new play that we are this day to act before you. Judge, therefore, whether this ought to be called a theft, or if it is not rather recovering what another's negligence has overlooked. For as to what these envious men allege, that some of our great men assist him, and are constantly writing with him; this, which they look upon as a mighty reproach, he regards as his greatest merit, that he has it in his power to please those, with whom you, and the whole people of Rome, are so much pleased; and whose services in war, in peace, and even in your private affairs, each one of you has used unreservedly, according to his need. As to what remains, do not expect now to hear from me the subject of the play; the two old men, who come on first, will partly explain it, and the rest will gradually appear in the representation. Do you, by a candid and impartial attention, encourage the poet to industry in writing?

# THE PLAY

## CHARACTERS IN THE PLAY

MICIO, an aged Athenian

DEMEA, his brother, father of Aeschinus and Ctesipho

SANNIO, a pimp

AESCHINUS, son of Demea, adopted by Micio

SYRUS, slave of Micio and Aeschinus

CTESIPHO, son of Demea

SOSTRATA, an Athenian lady

CANTHARA, an old woman, servant of Sostrata

GETA, slave of Sostrata

HEGIO, an old man of Athens

PAMPHILA, daughter of Sostrata

DROMO, slave of Micio

MUSIC GIRL

PARMENO, a slave

**SCENE:** A street in Athens in front of the houses of MICIO and SOSTRATA. The time is early morning

# ACT I

## SCENE I

[*Enter Micio from his house*]

MICIO: [*Calling within*] Storax! [To himself, as there is no answer] Well, Aeschinus didn't' return last night from supper, nor any of the servants who went to meet him. It is, indeed, a true saying: if you are absent anywhere, or chance to stay longer than ordinary, better those things happen to you which your wife says, or fancies in her resentment, than what indulgent parents are apt to suspect. Your wife, if you are out late, fancies you have picked up a girl, or a girl you, or that you are at the tavern, or amusing yourself somewhere, and that you make yourself quite happy, while she is uneasy and pines at home.

But for me now, what apprehensions am I under, because my son has not returned; how anxious, lest he may have caught cold, or had a fall, or broken some limb! Good gods! That a man should set his mind so much upon anything, as to allow it to become dearer to him than he is to himself! Nor is this boy, indeed, my son, but my brother's, one who is of a temperament very different from mine. Even from my youth, I have courted ease, and the quiet enjoyments of a town life, and, what men of pleasure count a happiness have always lived single. He again is quite the reverse of all this. He has lived in the country, being always sparing and laborious; he married, and had two sons. Of these, I have adopted the elder; bred him up from a child, kept him with me, and loved him as my own; he is now my whole delight, and what alone I hold dear; and I do all I can, too, that I may be equally dear to him. I give, I overlook things, I don't think it necessary to exert my authority on every occasion. In short, I have accustomed my son not to conceal from me those little extravagances natural to youth, which others are at so many pains to hide from their parents. For he who is accustomed to lie to, or deceive his father, will be more likely to cheat others. And I think it more prudent to hold children to their duty by the ties of kindness and honour, than by the restraints of fear. In this my brother and I differ widely, nor is he at all pleased with my manner. He often comes to me, loudly exclaiming, "What are you about, Micio? Why do you thus ruin the youth? Why does he drink? And why do you supply him with funds for all those extravagances? You indulge him too much in fine dress; you are quite silly in doing so." Why truly, he himself is much too severe, beyond what is either just or reasonable. And, in my judgment, he deceives himself greatly, to imagine that an authority established by force will be more lasting, or of greater weight, 'than one which is founded on friendship. For in this manner do I reason, and thus persuade myself to believe. He that does his duty from mere motives of fear will be upon his guard no longer than while he thinks there is danger of his being discovered, but if he can hope to escape notice, he returns to his natural bent; but where one is won over by kindness, he acts from inclination, strives to make a due return, and, present or absent, will be the same. This, indeed, is the part of a father, to accustom his son to do what is right, more from his own choice, than any fear of another; and here chiefly lies the difference between a father and a master. He who can't do this should admit that he doesn't know how to bring up children. But isn't this the very man of whom I was speaking? 'Tis the same; he seems vexed too, I can't think why. I believe, as usual, we shall have a quarrel. Demea, I am glad to see you so well.

## SCENE II

[*Enter Demea from the country*]

DEMEA: H'm! Just in time. You're the very man I was looking for.

MICIO: What makes you look so vexed?

DEMEA: Can you ask why? Do you know where our son Aeschinus is? Do you know now why I am vexed?

MICIO [*Aside*] Didn't I say it would be so? [*To Demea*] What has he done?

DEMEA: What has he done? He is ashamed of nothing and afraid of nobody and thinks no law binding upon him. I pass over his former escapades; what an outrage he has just now perpetrated!

MICIO: Why, what has he done?

DEMEA: He has broken open a street-door and made his way into a strange house, has beaten the master of the house and all his people nearly to death, and carried away a woman he's in love with. Everybody declares that it is a most shameful thing. As I was coming here, Micio, you don't know how many people told me this story; all Athens is full of it. If the boy needs an example, doesn't he see his brother working away in the country thriftily and soberly? He does nothing of this sort. Now Micio, when I say this to him, I say it to you, for you are letting him go to the bad.

MICIO: There never is anything so unfair as an ignorant man, who thinks that nothing can be right except what he does himself.

DEMEA: What do you mean by that?

MICIO: I mean, Demea, that you take a wrong view of this. Believe me, it is not a monstrous crime for a young man to indulge in wine and women; it isn't, really; nor yet to break open street-doors. If neither you nor I did such things, it was because poverty did not permit us to do them; you now are taking credit to yourself for not having done what you could not afford to do. This is quite wrong, for had we had the means, we should have done these things; and if you were a sensible man, you would let that son of yours do so now, while he is of an age for such follies, rather than that he should do them all the same when he ought to be too old for them, when at last he has had the pleasure of putting you underground.

DEMEA: By Jupiter, you make me wild! Not a monstrous crime for a young man to do so?

MICIO: Listen, and don't din this into my ears. You have given me your son to be mine by adoption; he has become my son. Now, Demea, if he does wrong, that is my affair; I shall have to bear most of the expenses. Suppose that he makes love, drinks wine, perfumes himself: I shall pay for it. Suppose he keeps a mistress: well, as long as I find it convenient, I shall let him have money for her; if I don't find it convenient, perhaps he will find her door shut against him. Now, if he has broken open a street-door, it will have to be mended; if he has torn any clothes, they must be sewn up again; and, thanks be to the gods, I can afford to have these things done, and thus far they do not weigh heavily upon me. The long and the short of it is, either leave off interfering, or choose someone to arbitrate between us. I can show that you are more to blame than I.

DEMEA: Oh, dear me! Learn to be a father from those who really know what it is!

MICIO: You are his father according to nature; but in care of him, I am.

DEMEA: As if you cared at all for him!

MICIO If you go on talking like that, I shall go away.

---

DEMEA: That you should act thus!

MICIO: How many times over am I to hear the same thing?

DEMEA: It is a matter of interest to me.

MICIO: So it is to me; but let us each look after our own part: you see to one brother, Demea, and I will see to the other; for if you look after both of them, -it is much the same thing as asking back the son you gave to me.

DEMEA: Oh, Micio!

MICIO: That's my view of the matter.

DEMEA: Well, well, if you like it, let him squander, waste, and go to the devil; it's nothing to me. And if I ever hear another word--

MICIO: Why, Demea, are you getting into a passion again?

DEMEA: Don't you believe me? Do I ask you to give me back the son I gave you? I own it is hard; I am not a stranger to him; it would not be surprising if I were to interfere-well, I leave off interfering. You wish me to look after one of my sons; very good, I am looking after him, and I am thankful to heaven that he is such a son as I should wish. That one of yours will find out some day how wrong he has been. I do not want to say anything worse about him. [*Demea departs*]

MICIO: [*To himself*] What he says is not all true, yet there is some truth in it, and I myself am vexed at it somewhat, though I wouldn't show him that I was sorry for it; for he is the sort of man that, to try to appease him I must be' careful to oppose and thwart him, and even then he does not take it kindly; but if I were to increase his anger or add fuel to it, why I should be as mad as he is. Yet, for all that, Aeschinus has not treated me quite properly by doing this. What courtesan is there in all Athens whom he has not been in love with, or to whom he has not made a present? Last of all, the other day, sick of them all, I believe, he said that he should like to marry. I hoped that he had sown his wild oats, and was glad of it; now, behold, he has begun afresh. But whatever it is that he has done, I should like to know about it and have a talk with him, if he's in the market place.

[*Micio departs towards the forum. A short time is supposed to elapse before the next Act*]

# ACT II

## SCENE I

[*Enter Aeschinus with a Music girl; Parmeno and other Slaves attend him. Sannio follows*]

SANNIO: My countrymen, I beseech you, help an injured and innocent man. Assist one who is helpless.

AESCHINUS: [*To the Girl*] Take it easy, stand still here now. Why do you look behind you? There's no danger; he will never lay a finger on you while I'm here.

SANNIO: I'll get her back, in spite of all of you.

AESCHINUS: [*To the Girl*] Scoundrel as he is, he won't risk getting another thrashing today!

SANNIO: Aeschinus, listen to me, that you mayn't say you didn't know my ways. I am a slave-dealer.
AESCHINUS: I know that you are.

SANNIO: But the most honourable in my business that there ever was. Now I don't care a straw for what you will plead in your defence--that you are sorry for having committed this outrage upon me. Mark me, I'll stand out for my lawful rights, and it will not be by words alone that you will pay for the harm you have done me by deeds. I know your excuses-- "Sorry it was done; will make an affidavit that you didn't deserve such ill-treatment," after I have been so shamefully misused!

AESCHINUS: [*To the Slaves*] Go on ahead quickly and open the door.

SANNIO: Then don't you pay any attention to what I say?

AESCHINUS: [*To the Girl*] Go into the house straightway.

SANNIO: But I won't let her go into the house.

AESCHINUS: Close up on that side, Parmeno; you are too far away; stand here close to him; there, that's where I want you to be. Now, mind you never take your eyes off mine, so that you may lose no time, when I give you the wink, in bringing your fist down on his jaw.

SANNIO: I should like him to try. [*Lays hold of the Girl*]

AESCHINUS: Here, mind what you're about. Let the girl go.

[*Parmeno hits Sannio in the face*]

SANNIO: Oh, shame!

AESCHINUS: [*To Sannio*] He'll do it again, if you don't take care.
[*Parmeno hits Sannio again*]

SANNIO: Oh, dear me!

AESCHINUS: I didn't wink to you to do it again; still, it's a fault on the right side. Now be off!

[*Parmeno takes the Girl into Micio's house*]

SANNIO: What's all this mean? Are you king in these parts, Aeschinus?

AESCHINUS: If I were, you would meet your deserts.

SANNIO: What have you to do with me?

AESCHINUS: Nothing.

SANNIO: What? Do you know who I am?

AESCHINUS: I don't want to know.

SANNIO: Have I meddled with any of your property?

AESCHINUS: It would have been the worse for you if you had.

SANNIO: Why should you have my slave that I bought and paid for? Answer me.

AESCHINUS: You had better not abuse me in front of my own house; for if you go on making yourself a nuisance, I'll have you taken into the house and flogged there within an inch of your life.

SANNIO: Flog me, a free man!
AESCHINUS: That's what will be done.

SANNIO: O villain; and this is the place where they say that all men are free alike!

AESCHINUS: Now then, master slave-dealer, if you have quite done storming, be good enough to listen to me.

SANNIO: Have I been storming against you, or you against me?

AESCHINUS: Never mind that, come to the point.

SANNIO: What point? Where am I to come to?

AESCHINUS: Are you ready for me to tell you about your concern in this matter?

SANNIO: I am willing, provided that I get some of my rights.

AESCHINUS: Ho! Ho! Here's a slave-dealer bids me talk righteously!

SANNIO: I am a slave-dealer, I confess it, the ruin of all young men; I am a liar and a scoundrel; but still I have never done you any wrong.

AESCHINUS: No, that's the one thing that's left for you to do.

SANNIO: Pray, Aeschinus, return to what you began about.

AESCHINUS: You bought this girl for twenty minae; you shall be paid the same sum, and much good may it do you.

SANNIO: What if I refuse to sell her to you? Will you make me?

AESCHINUS: Not at all.

SANNIO: I was afraid that you would.

AESCHINUS: I don't believe that she is saleable, for I claim her as a free woman as the law directs in such cases. Now make your choice, whether you will take the money or think what defence you can make. I leave you to your reflections here, master slave-dealer, until I return. [*Aeschinus goes into the house*]

SANNIO: [*To himself*] Almighty Jove! I don't wonder at men being driven mad by outrage. He has dragged me out of my house, beaten me, and carried off my slave-girl against my will; he has bestowed more than five hundred blows upon me; and now, as the reward of his crimes, he expects to get her for no more than I gave for her. [*Ironically*] Well, since he has treated me so well, so be it; he has a right, no doubt. Why, I'm quite willing, provided he pays me the money for her. But I'm talking nonsense. When I say that I gave so much for her, he will straightway have witnesses ready to prove that I have sold her to him, and the money will be all moonshine. He'll say, "Call again tomorrow." Well, I could put up with that, too, if only he would pay, in spite of the injustice of it. But I know how things are: if you ply my trade, you must submit to outrages from young gentlemen and hold your tongue. I shall never be paid; it's no use for me to make these calculations.

## SCENE II

[*Enter Syrus from Micio's house*]

SYRUS: [*To his master within*] Say no more; I'll see the man myself; I'll make him glad to take the money, and declare that he has been well treated. [*To Sannio*] What's this I hear, Sannio, about your having been fighting with my master?

SANNIO: I never saw a. more one-sided fight than that between him and me today, for I got beaten, and he beat me till we were both tired out.

SYRUS: Well, it was all your fault.

SANNIO: What ought I to have done?

SYRUS: You ought to have made allowances for the young gentleman.

SANNIO: "What more could I have done; haven't I allowed him to hit me in the face?

SYRUS: Come, you understand what I mean. Sometimes the most profitable think we can do is not to be over keen after one's money.

SANNIO: The deuce it is!

SYRUS: You great goose, if you don't insist upon your rights just now, and let the young gentleman have his way, you surely cannot fear that you will not profit by so doing in the long run?

SANNIO: A bird in the hand is worth two in the bush.

SYRUS: You will never make a fortune; get along with you, Sannio, you don't understand how to entice men on.

SANNIO: I believe that is the best way, but I never was so cunning as not to prefer to get what I could in ready money.

SYRUS: Come, I know what you're thinking of; as if twenty minae made any difference to you, in comparison with doing my master a favour. Besides, they say you are on the point (of setting sail for Cyprus.
SANNIO: [Aside] The devil!

SYRUS: That you have bought up a large cargo for that place, and hired a ship. Come, I know you're in two minds about it; when you return, I hope, you can still settle this affair.

SANNIO: I'm not going to stir from this place. [Aside] Confound it! This was what they were relying upon when they began.

SYRUS: [*Aside*] He's afraid. I've put a spoke in his wheel.

SANNIO: [*Aside*] What villainy! See how he has caught me just in the very nick of time. I've bought lots of slave-girls, and other merchandise besides, which I am going to take to Cyprus. Unless I get them there in time for the fair, it will be a dead loss. But if I drop this business now, and begin it again when I return from Cyprus, all's lost; the whole thing will have blown over. They will say, "Why didn't you come into court before? Why did you let him do it? Where were you?" So it is better to lose the money than either to wait here so long or to try to get it when I come back.

SYRUS: Well, have you finished reckoning up what you expect to make by your voyage?

SANNIO: Is this the way that Aeschinus ought to behave? To think that he should try to do such a thing; to expect to take this girl from me by main force.

SYRUS: [*Aside*] He is giving way. [Aloud] Now, Sannio, I've only one proposal to make; see whether it suits you. Rather than risk winning or losing it all, split the difference. He'll scrape up ten minae somehow.

SANNIO: Confound it, am I now to lose the principal as well as the interest? Has he no shame? He has loosened all my teeth; besides, my head is all bumps with his knocks; and is he going to cheat me as well? I won't leave this place.

SYRUS: Please yourself. Anything else before I go?

---

SANNIO: Yes, damn it! I beg you, Syrus, no matter what has been done, rather than go to law about it, let me have the bare price that I gave for the girl, anyway, my good Syrus. I know that you have not as yet profited by my friendship, but hereafter you will find me mindful of your kindness, and grateful.

SYRUS: I'll do my best. But I see Ctesipho there; he's pleased at getting his mistress.

SANNIO: What are you going to do about my request?

SYRUS: Wait a bit.


## SCENE III

[Enter Ctesipho, overjoyed]

CTESIPHO: [To himself] One is always pleased to be done a good turn in time of need, by anybody; much more pleasant is it when one whose duty it is does one good. My dear brother, what need is there for me to praise you now? I am quite sure that, however grandly I spoke of you; it would fall short of your real merit. I think that I have this great advantage over everybody else, that no one has so noble a gentleman for a brother.

SYRUS: Good day, Ctesipho.
CTESIPHO: Oh, Syrus, where is Aeschinus?

SYRUS: [Pointing to the house] There he is; he's waiting for you in the house.

CTESIPHO: Aha!

SYRUS: What is the matter?

CTESIPHO: The matter! Why, Syrus, I owe him my life for what he has done, the delightful fellow, who has thought nothing of his own disgrace compared with my interests. He has taken upon his own shoulders all the scandal, reproach, intrigue, and blame that belongs to me. He could do nothing more. What's that noise at the door?

SYRUS: Wait; he himself is coming out


## SCENE IV

[*Enter Aeschinus from Micio's house*]

AESCHINUS: Where's that scoundrel?

SANNIO: [*Aside*] He is seeking me; is he bringing any money out with him? Confusion! I don't see any.

AESCHINUS: Oh, well met, Ctesipho; the very man I was looking for! How goes it? All is safely finished, so lay aside your gloom.

CTESIPHO: I do indeed lay it aside, because I have you for my brother. Oh, Aeschinus, my own brother, I am ashamed to praise you more to your face, for fear you should think I do it to flatter rather than because I am grateful to you.

AESCHINUS: Go on, goose; as if we didn't understand each other, Ctesipho. What I am sorry for is that we very nearly learned it too late, and that matters very nearly went so far that all the people in the world could not have helped you, if they had wanted.

CTESIPHO: I was ashamed to tell you.

AESCHINUS: That is folly, not shame. That you should have been on the point of leaving your native land all because of a trifle of money like that! Disgraceful! May heaven save us from such a fate!

CTESIPHO: I was wrong.

AESCHINUS: [To Syrus] And, pray, what terms does Sannio propose to us now?

SYRUS: He is quite reasonable now.

AESCHINUS: I'll go to the market place and pay him. Ctesipho, you go into the house to the girl.

SANNIO: Syrus, help me.

SYRUS: [To Aeschinus] Let us be going, for this man is in a hurry to go to Cyprus.

SANNIO: Yes; but not so much of a hurry as you wish. I have plenty of time to wait here.

SYRUS: You shall be paid, never fear.

SANNIO: But see that he pays me in full.

SYRUS: He will pay you in full; only hold your tongue and follow me this way.

SANNIO: I am following you.

*[Aeschinus and Sannio depart. Syrus is detained by Ctesipho]*

CTESIPHO: I say, Syrus.
SYRUS: What is it?

CTESIPHO: I entreat you, close your account with that loathsome
villain as soon as may be, for fear that if he be made angrier than he is, my father may somehow get wind of this and I be ruined forever.

SYRUS: You won't be, be of good cheer; go into the house and take your pleasure with her in the meantime, and tell them to lay the table for us and get things ready for dinner; as soon as I have transacted the business I will come home again with something to cook.

CTESIPHO: Do so, I pray you; after our success we will have a jolly day.

*[Ctesipho goes into Micio's house; Syrus hurries after Aeschinus]*

# ACT III

## SCENE I

*[Enter Sostrata from her house, followed by Canthara]*

SOSTRATA: Pray, my dear nurse, what will happen now?

CANTHARA: What will happen, do you ask? All will go right, I hope.

SOSTRATA: My dear, her pains are just beginning to come upon her.

CANTHARA: You are as much afraid as if you had never seen a child born, never borne a child yourself.

SOSTRATA: Wretched woman that I am, I have no one, we are all alone, and Geta is not, here. No one to send to the midwife, or to fetch Aeschinus.

CANTHARA: Heavens, he will be here soon, for he never misses a day without calling.

SOSTRATA: He is Thy only protection against my miseries.

CANTHARA: Mistress, after what has happened, things could not have turned out better than they have; since the girl has been violated, it is well that her seducer is such a fine young man, such a 'fine character and spirit, and belonging to so noble a family.

SOSTRATA: What you say is true; may the gods preserve him for us.

# SCENE II

*[Enter Geta, hurrying in great excitement]*

GETA: *[To himself]* Now this is a matter in which, if all mankind gave all the advice they could, and tried to find a remedy for this misfortune which has befallen me and my mistress and the daughter, they could give us no help. Oh, dear me! So many things suddenly threaten us on every side, from which there is no escape: violence, poverty, injustice, loneliness, disgrace. What a time we live in! What crimes are committed! What a vile race it is! What a wicked man he is!

SOSTRATA: *[Aside to Canthara]* Oh, dear me, why do I see Geta frightened and hurrying like this?

GETA: Neither honour, nor his plighted word, nor pity could hold him back or turn him from his purpose, nor yet the thought that the girl whom he had outraged was about to become a mother.

SOSTRATA: *[Aside to Canthara]* I don't quite understand what he's saying.

CANTHARA: Pray, Sostrata, let us go nearer to him.

*[They approach]*

GETA: Oh, dear! I am so hot with anger that I am scarcely in my right mind. I should like nothing better than to meet the whole of that household, that I might vent my rage upon them now, while the pain is fresh. I should not care how much I was punished if only I could take a thorough revenge upon them. First of all, I would choke the life out of the old man who begat the monster; then Syrus, the instigator of his wickedness! Oh, how I would mangle him! First, I would take him by the middle,

139

hoist him up aloft, and bring his head down on to the ground, so that his brains bespattered the road. As for the young man himself, I would first tear his eyes out, and then fling him down a cliff headfirst. The rest I would fall upon, beat them, dash them down, smash them, overthrow them. But why don't I tell my mistress this bad news straightway?

SOSTRATA: [To Canthara] Let us call him back. Geta!

GETA: Now, whoever you are, let me go my way.

SOSTRATA: It is I, Sostrata.

GETA: [Turning round] Where is she? It is you yourself that I am seeking, my mistress, it is you that I want; indeed, it's fortune that you have fallen in with me.

SOSTRATA: What is it? Why are you in a flutter?

GETA: Oh, dear!

CANTHARA: Why are you in such a hurry, my good Geta? Wait and get your breath.

GETA: We are utterly—

SOSTRATA: What does that "utterly" mean?

GETA: Ruined. All's over with us.

SOSTRATA: Tell me, I beseech you, what the matter is?

GETA: By this time--

SOSTRATA: What is "by this time," Geta?

---

GETA: Aeschinus--

SOSTRATA: Well, what of him?

GETA: Is a stranger to our family.
SOSTRATA: What? Good gracious! Why so?

GETA: He has begun an amour with another woman.

SOSTRATA: Oh, miserable woman that I am!

GETA: And he makes no secret of it, but has carried her off from the slave-dealer in the sight of all men.

SOSTRATA: Is this proved to be true?

GETA: True! I saw it, Sostrata, with these very eyes.

SOSTRATA: Oh, poor wretch that I am! What is one now to believe, or whom should one believe? That our Aeschinus should have done this! He that was our very life, our only hope and help; he who used to swear that without her he could not live for one day; who used to say that he would set her child in his father's lap, and entreat him to let him marry her.

GETA: Mistress, dry your tears, and consider what we ought to do in this case. Are we to put up with his conduct, or shall we tell someone about it?

CANTHARA: Good gracious, man, are you in your right mind? Do you think that ours is a tale for anyone to hear?

GETA: I myself am against telling it. In the first place, what he has done shows that he doesn't care for us, and now, if we publish our story, I am quite sure he will contradict it, and then you will risk your good name and your daughter's prospects in life. Secondly, even if he admits the truth, of our story, there's no point to letting him marry your daughter, since he loves another woman. So, in either case, you must hold your tongue.

SOSTRATA: Ah, but I won't; not a bit.

GETA: What will you do?

SOSTRATA: Publish the whole story.

CANTHARA: But, my dear Sostrata, just think what you are doing.

SOSTRATA: Matters can't be worse for us than they are; first of all she has no dowry, and then, too, her honour, her second dowry, is lost. I can't give her to anyone as a maid. If he disowns her, all that I shall have left to prove my story is the ring that he lost, which I have. Finally, as I am aware in my own mind that there has been nothing to blame in my conduct, Geta, that she has not received any money or anything else as compensation, and that neither of us has acted dishonourably, I'll try what the law will do for us.

GETA: Well, well, I agree; your suggestion is better.

SOSTRATA: Run as fast as you can and tell the whole story from the very beginning to Hegio, who was my Simulus' greatest friend, and was very fond of us.

GETA: Indeed, no one besides him takes any notice of us now.

*[Geta departs]*

SOSTRATA: My good Canthara, do you haste to bring a midwife, so that she may be at hand when we want her.

*[Canthara departs; Sostrata goes into her house]*

## SCENE III

*[Enter Demea, much troubled)*

DEMEA: [To himself] Confusion! I have heard that my son Ctesipho took part with Aeschinus in this abduction. It would, indeed, be the last straw for me, if he is able to seduce the son who really is good for something, into mischief. Where am I to look for him? I suppose he has been carried off into some low dive; that profligate has led him away, I'm sure. Why, there I see Syrus going along. I will soon make out from him where he is. And yet Syrus is one of that gang; if he sees that I am looking for Ctesipho, the scoundrel will never tell me where he is. I won't let him see that I want to know.

*[Enter Syrus with a basket of provisions]*

SYRUS: [*To himself*] We told the old gentleman the whole story just as it happened from the outset. I never saw anyone better pleased.

DEMEA: [*Aside*] Great Jupiter, that the man should be such a fool!

SYRUS: He highly commended his son, and thanked me for having suggested the plan to him.

DEMEA: [*Aside*] I'm fit to burst with anger.

SYRUS: He counted out the money then and there, and gave us half a mina besides for our expenses. That has been laid out according to my ideas.

DEMEA: [*Aside*] Oh, yes, this is the man to entrust your business to, if you want it looked after properly! [*Advancing*]

SYRUS: Why, Demea, I didn't see you; how goes it?

DEMEA: How goes it! I am astounded at your proceedings.

SYRUS: Silly enough they are; to speak plainly, ridiculous. [*He goes to the door and hands his basket to the cooks within*] Dromo, clean the fish all but that big eel; let him play in the water a little while; he shall be boned when I come back, but I don't want him killed till then.

DEMEA: Such atrocities as these!

SYRUS: Indeed, I don't approve of them myself, and I often cry out. [*To the cooks within*] Stephanie, mind you soak that salt fish thoroughly.

DEMEA: Good heavens! Is it his object to ruin his son, or does he thinks that it would be to his credit? Oh, dear me, I already seem to see the day when he will run away somewhere and enlist.

SYRUS: Indeed, Demea, this is true wisdom, not to see only what stares you in the face, but also what is to come.

DEMEA: Now then, is that music girl in your house now?

SYRUS: Yes, she's within.

DEMEA: Pray, is he going to keep her in his own house?

SYRUS: I believe he is; he's crazy enough to do it. .

DEMEA: That such things should be done!

SYRUS: All the fault lies with his father's silly good-nature and criminal weakness.

DEMEA: I am ashamed of my brother and grieve for him.

SYRUS: Demea, I say this before your face as I would say it behind your back; there is too much, far too much difference between you and your brother. What a man you are, every inch a sage! He's a stupid fool! Would you have let your son do this?

DEMEA: Would I have let him? Wouldn't I have smelt a rat six months before he set about doing anything!

SYRUS: You need not tell me how sharp-sighted you are.

DEMEA: I hope I shall always be as sharp as I am now.

SYRUS: Each son is as his father would have him be.

DEMEA: What of mine? Have you seen him today?

SYRUS: Your son? [*Aside*] I'll send this old man off to the country. [*Aloud*] I think he's been working on your farm in the country for some time now.

DEMEA: Are you quite sure that he is there?

SYRUS: Why, I myself saw him off.

DEMEA: Capital! I was afraid he might be hanging about here.

SYRUS: And a fine rage he was in.

DEMEA: What about?

SYRUS: He quarreled with his brother in the market place about this music girl

DEMEA: Indeed?

SYRUS: Yes, he didn't mince matters; he came upon us all of a sudden when the money was being paid, and began to cry out, "Oh, Aeschinus, that you should behave so scandalously! That you should disgrace our family by such escapades!"

DEMEA: Oh, I weep with joy.

SYRUS: "It is not only this money," said he, "but your life that you are throwing away."

DEMEA: Long may he live; he, I hope, is a chip off the old block.

SYRUS: Quite.

DEMEA: Syrus, he's full of those wise saws.

SYRUS: Right He had someone at home to learn them from.

DEMEA: I took care of that: I never lose an opportunity of instruction; I accustom him to virtue; in fact, I bid him look into all men's lives as into a mirror, and make others serve as examples to himself. I say to him, "Practise this."

SYRUS: Excellent!

DEMEA: "Avoid that."

SYRUS: A wise education!

DEMEA: I say, "Men praise this."

SYRUS: That's the way to teach.

DEMEA: "They disapprove of that."

SYRUS: You couldn't do better.

DEMEA: And moreover-

SYRUS: [*Interrupting*] Indeed, I have no leisure now to listen to you any longer, Demea. I have got some fish after my own heart; I must take care that they're not spoiled; for with us, Demea, this is as great a crime as it is with you, not to practise those noble precepts which you have just told us of, and I do my best to give my fellow-servants instruction after the same fashion, saying, "This is too salt"; "this is over-cooked"; "this is not properly cleaned"; "this is as it should be"; "bear this in mind another time." In fact, I bid them look into the dishes, Demea, as into a mirror, and tell them what they ought to do. I am aware that you think these pursuits of ours silly; but what are you to do? You must deal with a man according to his character. Have you anything further for me? .

DEMEA: Only to pray that heaven may give you all better sense.

SYRUS: Are you going to the country?

DEMEA: Straightway.

SYRUS: Yes, indeed, what should you do here, where, if you did give good advice, no one would follow it. *[Syrus goes into the house]*

DEMEA: [*To himself*] Now I'm off to the country, because the boy I came here about has himself gone there: he is my only care; he belongs to me. As my brother wishes to have it so, he may look after the other one himself. [Looking down the street] But who is that I see in the distance? Is it not my fellow-tribesman, Hegio? If my eyes don't deceive me, it is be, indeed. Now there's a man who has been my friend from his youth up.

Good heavens! We are not rich in citizens of his sort; he is of the good and honourable old school. It will be long ere the state suffers any injury from him. How pleased I am; I find life worth living even at the present day, when I see some remnants of that race still surviving. I'll wait for him here, that I may greet him and talk with him.

## SCENE IV

[*Enter Hegio and Geta conversing*]

HEGIO: By the immortal gods, this is a disgraceful action! What is it that you tell me?

GETA: The truth.

HEGIO: That such an ungentlemanly act should come from one of that family! By Jove, Aeschinus, you have shown little of your father's character in this!

DEMEA: [*Aside*] Of course, he must have heard about this music girl; the thing grieves him, though he is a stranger; but his father thinks nothing of it. Oh dear! I wish he were somewhere close by here, and could hear this.

HEGIO: Unless they behave properly, they shall not get away with it.

GETA: Hegio, our only hope is in you; we have no one beside you; you are our patron, our father. The old man, on his deathbed, entrusted us to your care. If you forsake us, we're lost.

HEGIO: Don't speak of such a thing. I won't desert you, nor could I, without disloyalty to my friend.

DEMEA: [*Aside*] I'll accost him. [*Aloud*] Hegio, my very best respects.

HEGIO: Well, you're the very man I was seeking; good day, Demea.

DEMEA: What is the matter?

HEGIO: That elder son of yours, Aeschinus, whom your brother adopted, has not behaved like a good man or like a gentleman.

DEMEA: What has he done?

HEGIO: You know my friend Simulus; he was about our own age?

DEMEA: Of course I knew him.

HEGIO: He has seduced his daughter.

DEMEA: Gracious heavens!

HEGIO: Wait, Demea, you haven't yet heard the worst part of it.

DEMEA: Why, is there anything worse?

HEGIO: Worse, indeed; for this might have been excused somehow; he was excited by the darkness, by passion, by wine, by youth; it is human nature. Now when he learned what he had done, he went of his own accord to the maiden's mother; he wept, prayed, and implored her, giving his word of honour and swearing that he would make her his wife. He was pardoned, the affair was hushed up, his word was believed. The girl became pregnant through his violence; this is the tenth month. Now, if you please, my young gentleman has carried off this music girl to live with him, and has deserted the other.

DEMEA: Are you sure of the truth of what you say?

HEGIO: There is the girl's mother, the girl herself, the thing itself; besides, here is Geta, not a bad slave as slaves go, and a hard-working one; he supports them, he alone maintains the whole household. Take him, put him in chains, and enquire into the matter.

GETA: Nay, put me to the torture if that isn't the truth, Demea. Moreover, he won't deny it; bring him into my presence.

DEMEA: [Aside] I am ashamed. I don't know what to do, or what answer to give to him.

PAMPHILA: [Within Sostrata's house] Oh, dear me! I am in agonies. Juno, thou that bringest babes to light, save me, I beseech thee!

HEGIO: What's that? Can she be in labour?

GETA: She is indeed, Hegio.

HEGIO: Well, Demea, she now appeals to you to do of your own free will what the law can make you do. I hope that you will behave as becomes you in this matter; but, Demea, if you do not choose to do so, I will fight as hard as I can to protect her, and him who is gone, He was my kinsman; we were always together, both at home and in the wars; we endured bitter poverty together, and therefore I will struggle, and strive, and go to law, and lay down my very life sooner than desert his family.

DEMEA: I will talk to my brother, Hegio.

HEGIO: But, Demea, mind that you consider this point. You and your brother are powerful, rich, prosperous, and noble; but in proportion as life is easy to you, all the more ought you to judge things rightly and act righteously, if you wish to be esteemed honourable men. [He turns towards Sostrata's door]

DEMEA: Come back, come back; whatever is right shall be done.

HEGIO: That's what you ought to do. Geta, take me into the house to Sostrata.

[Hegio and Geta go inside]

DEMEA: [To himself] These things have not come to pass for want of my warnings. Please heaven; this may be the end of it all! But this excessive indulgence will certainly lead to some terrible mischief in the end. I will go and look for my brother, and pour all this into his ears. [Demea departs towards the forum]


## SCENE V

[Re-enter Hegio]

HEGIO: [To Sostrata within] Be of good cheer, Sostrata, and console the girl as well as you can. I will see Micio, if he's in the market place, and tell him the whole story, from beginning to end; then, if he is inclined to do his duty, he may do it; but if not, he shall give me his answer, and then I'll know without delay what steps I am to take. [Hegio departs towards the forum]

# ACT IV

## SCENE I

*[Enter Ctesipho and Syrus from Micio's house]*

CTESIPHO: Did you say that my father went off to the country?

SYRUS: Long ago.

CTESIPHO: Pray tell me about it.

SYRUS: He is at his farm, and just about now, I fancy, he's engaged on some piece of work.

CTESIPHO: I trust so. I hope that, without doing himself any serious harm, he may so tire himself out that he won't be able to get out of bed for the whole of these next three days.

SYRUS: SO be it; and better than that, if possible.

CTESIPHO: Yes; for I am desperately eager to pass all this day as I have begun it, in enjoyment; and the reason why I dislike this farm so much is that it is so near Athens. Now, if it had been further off, night would have overtaken him before he could have returned here. As it is, when he doesn't see me there, he will run back here, I am quite sure; he'll ask me where I have been; he'll say, "I haven't seen you the whole of this day." What answer am I to make?

SYRUS: Doesn't anything come into your head?

CTESIPHO: Nothing whatever.

SYRUS: So much the worse for you. Have you no dependent, no friend, rib guest from abroad?

CTESIPHO: Yes, I have; what then?

SYRUS: Can't you say that you were attending to them?

CTESIPHO: When I wasn't attending to them? No, that won't do.

SYRUS: Yes, it will.

CTESIPHO: In the daytime, I grant you; but, Syrus, if I pass the night here, what reason can I give?

SYRUS: Dear me! How I wish it was the fashion to attend to one's friends by night as well as by day! But don't you trouble yourself, I know his ways perfectly; when he is at his angriest I can make him as quiet as a lamb.

CTESIPHO: How do you manage it?

SYRUS: He likes to hear your praises; I make a regular god of you in his mind. I tell him about your virtues.

CTESIPHO: My virtues?

SYRUS: Yes, yours; and straightway the tears roll down his cheeks for joy, as if he was a child. But look out!

CTESIPHO: What is it?

SYRUS: Talk of the devil!

CTESIPHO: Is it my father?

SYRUS: His very self.

CTESIPHO: O Syrus! What are we to do?

SYRUS: Run indoors directly, and I will see after him.

CTESIPHO: If he asks you, mind, you haven't seen me anywhere; do you hear?

SYRUS: Can't you hold your tongue?

[*Ctesipho goes inside*]


## SCENE II

[*Enter Demea*]

DEMEA: [*To himself*] Indeed I am an unlucky man; first of all I can't find my brother anywhere in the world, and besides that, while I was looking for my son, I saw a labourer from my farm who says that my son is not in the country. I don't know what to do.

CTESIPHO: [*Aside to Syrus from the house*] Syrus!

SYRUS: [*Aside to Ctesipho*] What's the matter?

CTESIPHO: [*Aside to Syrus*] Is he after me?

SYRUS: [Aside to Ctesipho] Yes.

CTESIPHO: [*Aside to Syrus*] I am lost!

SYRUS: [*Aside to Ctesipho*] No, keep your heart up.

DEMEA: What a mass of disaster this is! I can't get a right

understanding of it, except on the supposition that I was born for nothing else but to endure miseries. I am the first to become aware of the misfortunes of the family: I learn the truth of them first; then, too, I am the first to bring the bad news to Micio; and I suffer alone for all that is done.

SYRUS: [*Aside*] He makes me laugh saying that he was the first to know, when he's the only man who knows nothing about it.

DEMEA: Now I've come back, I'll see whether my brother has come home.

CTESIPHO: [*Aside to Syrus from the house*] Syrus, pray take care he does not blunder straight in here.  .

SYRUS: [*Aside to Ctesipho*] Can't you be quiet. I'll take care.

CTESIPHO: [*Aside to Syrus*] I won't ever trust you to do that today; I'll lock myself in some room with the girl, that'll be the safest thing to do.

SYRUS: [*Aside to Ctesipho*] Come, I'll send him away.

DEMEA: Why, there's that scoundrel Syrus.

SYRUS: [*Pretending not to see Demea*] No, by heaven! If this sort of thing goes on, nobody can stay in this house. I should like to know how many masters I have; what misery this is!

DEMEA: What's he babbling about? What does he want? What are you saying, my good man? Is my brother at home?

SYRUS: What the devil do you mean by your "good man"? I am done for!

DEMEA: What's the matter with you?

---

SYRUS: The matter! Why, Ctesipho has thrashed me and that music girl almost to death.

DEMEA: Eh! What's that you tell me?

SYRUS: Why, see how he has split open my lip.

DEMEA: What did he do it for?

SYRUS: He says that it was by my advice that she was bought.

DEMEA: Didn't you say just now that you had seen him off to the country?

SYRUS: So I did, but after that he came back raving mad, and had no pity. He should have been ashamed to beat an old man like me; why, I carried him in my arms when he was only so big.

DEMEA: Well done, Ctesipho, you take after your father. Come, I count you a man.

SYRUS: What, do you praise him for it? Nay, if he is wise, he'll keep his fists to himself for the future.

DEMEA: He did bravely.

SYRUS: Oh, very bravely, to beat a wretched girl, and me, a slave, who dared not hit him back. Mighty bravely, indeed!

DEMEA: He could not have done better; like me, he saw that you were at the bottom of all this business. But is my brother at home?

SYRUS: No, he isn't.

DEMEA: I wonder where I can find him.

SYRUS: I know where he is, but I'll never tell you the place today.

DEMEA: Eh, what's that you say?

SYRUS: Just that.

DEMEA: You will have your head broken in a minute.

SYRUS: Well, I don't know the man's name, but I know where the place is.

DEMEA: Then tell me where the place is.

SYRUS: Do you know that colonnade at the butcher's shop down the street?

DEMEA: Of course I do.

SYRUS: When you've passed that, go straight up the street; when you've come there, there's a hill leading downwards; down that you go, and then there is a chapel on this side; [pointing] close by that there is a lane.

DEMEA: [*Looking*] Where?

SYRUS: [*Pointing*] There, where the great wild fig tree stands.

DEMEA: I know.

SYRUS: Go that way.

DEMEA: But that lane is no thoroughfare.

SYRUS: True, by Jove! Why, what a fool I must be! I have made a mistake. You must come back to the colonnade again; indeed, this is a much shorter way, and less chance of your missing it. Do you know that house there that belongs to the rich Cratinus?

DEMEA: Yes, I know it.

SYRUS: When you have passed it, turn to the left, go straight on that way till you come to Diana's temple, then to the right. Before you come to the city gate, just by the pond, there's a pounding-mill, and opposite a carpenter's shop; that's where he is.

DEMEA: What is he doing there?

SYRUS: He has ordered some benches to he made with oak legs, to stand the sun.

DEMEA: [*Sneering*] For you to lie upon and drink. Very well; I had better be off to him. [*Demea departs*]

SYRUS: Off with you, in heaven's name! I'll work you today as you deserve, you old fossil! [*Reflecting*] It's very wrong of Aeschinus not to come; our dinner is being spoiled. Ctesipho is thinking of nothing but his love; I must look out for myself I'll go in and pick out the choicest morsel of all for myself, and then I'll linger over my wine for the rest of the day. [*He goes into the house*]

## SCENE III

[*Enter Micio and Hegio, conversing*]

MICIO: Hegio, I don't see anything in this for which I deserve such high praise. I am only doing my duty; I am repairing the fault which we have committed; unless you used to reckon me among those who think that you are doing them an injury and abuse you if you complain of the wrong they have done you. Do you thank me because I don't act thus?

HEGIO: Oh, not at all; I never thought of you otherwise than as you are. But, Micio, I pray you, come with me to the girl's mother, and tell her yourself what you have told me, that all this suspicion arose on account of Aeschinus' brother and his music girl--

MICIO: Well, if you think it right, or that it needs doing, let us go.

HEGIO; You are right, for you will cheer up the woman, who is wasting away with sorrow and wretchedness, and you will have done your duty; still, if you don't wish to, I myself will tell her what you said.

MICIO: No, I'll go.

HEGIO: You are right. Somehow all those who are unsuccessful in life are prone to suspicion; they take everything as an insult, and believe that they are being slighted because they are helpless; so you are more likely to win their pardon if you defend yourself in person before them.

MICIO: What you say is true and proper.

HEGIO: Then come this way after me into the house.

MICIO: With all my heart. [*They go into Sostrata's house*)

# SCENE IV

*[Enter Aeschinus, much troubled]*

AESCHINUS: *[To himself]* I am in terrible distress; so much trouble has come upon me all of a sudden that I don't know what to do with myself or how to act My limbs quake with fear; my mind is stupefied with dread; my heart can form no plan. Heavens! How can I get myself out of this mess? I have become gravely suspected, and on very good grounds. Sostrata believes that I have bought this music girl for myself. The old woman told me this; she was going to fetch a midwife when I saw her. I straightway went to her and asked her how Pamphila was, whether her confinement was at hand and that was why she was fetching the midwife. She cried out, "Be off with you, Aeschinus; you have fooled us long enough; you have deceived us long enough with your fine professions." "Eh," says I, "pray what is all this?" "Goodbye" says she, "keep the girl you like best" I saw straightway what the women suspected, but still I restrained myself, for fear of telling that old chatterbox anything about my brother, and letting out the whole story. Now, what am I to do? Shall I tell them that the girl is my brother's mistress? That secret must not be breathed to anyone. And never mind that, for I think the secret may be kept; but I fear they would not believe the truth; so many circumstances point to the other as the real story. I myself carried off the girl; I paid the money for her; she was brought home to my house. I admit that I was wrong in that matter, not to have told my father the whole story of my love, and wrung permission from him to marry her. Hitherto I have been idling; now then, Aeschinus, my man, wake up. Now, first of all, I will go to the women and clear my character. Let me go up to the door. Oh, dear! I am always in a fright when I begin to knock at this door. *[Knocking]* Ho, there! It is Aeschinus. Open the door quick, somebody. Here is somebody coming out; I will stand aside here.

# SCENE V

[*Enter Micio from Sostrata's house*]

MICIO: [*To Sostrata within*) Do as I tell you, Sostrata; I will see Aeschinus, that he may know what has been done. But who is that who knocked?

AESCHINUS: [*Aside*] Heavens, it's my father! Confuion!

MICIO: Aeschinus!

AESCHINUS: [*Aside*] What is he doing here?

MICIO: Was it you who knocked at this door? [*Aside*] He doesn't answer. Why shouldn't I play with him for a while? It's right, seeing that he never chose to tell me anything about this. [*Aloud*) Do you give me no answer?

AESCHINUS: It wasn't that door, as far as I know.

MICIO: Indeed! I was wondering what business you could have here. [*Aside*] He blushes; all is well.

AESCHINUS: Tell me, pray, father, what business you have there.

MICIO: I have none. A friend just now brought me away from the market place as a witness.

AESCHINUS: What for?

MICIO: I'll tell you. Some poverty-stricken women live here; I don't suppose that you know them, indeed, I am quite sure you don't, for they have only lately moved into this house.

AESCHINUS: Well, what then?

MICIO: There is a young girl and her mother.

AESCHINUS: Yes, go on.

MICIO: The young girl has lost her father. This friend of mine is her next of kin, and is compelled by the law to marry her.

AESCHINUS: [*Aside*] The devil!

MICIO: [*Overhearing*] What's the matter?

AESCHINUS: Oh, nothing. I am all right. Go on.

MICIO: He is come to take her away with him, for he lives at Miletus.

AESCHINUS: What? To take the girl away with him?

MICIO: Yes.

AESCHINUS: What? All the way to Miletus?

MICIO: Just so.

AESCHINUS: [*Aside*] I feel as if I should faint. [*To Micio*] And what of the women? What do they say?

MICIO: What do you suppose they would say? Nothing at all. The mother did, indeed, make up a story that the girl had had a child by somebody else, some man or other, she didn't tell his name, and said that he came first, and that the girl ought not to marry my friend.

AESCHINUS: Well, don't you think that she was right to ask this?

MICIO: No.

AESCHINUS: What? "No?" And, father, is this man going to take her away?

MICIO: Why shouldn't he take her away?

AESCHINUS: Father, you have acted harshly and pitilessly, and even, to be plain', ungentlemanly.

MICIO: Why?

AESCHINUS: Do you ask me why? What do you suppose must be the feelings of that poor fellow, her former lover, who, unhappy man, perhaps is still desperately fond of her, when he has to stand by and see her carried off before his face and taken out of his sight? Father, it is a shameful thing to do.

MICIO: On what grounds do you say that? Who betrothed her to him? Who gave her to him? When was she married? Whom did she marry? Who gave his consent to these proceedings? Why did the man marry a girl who belonged to another?

AESCHINUS: Why, was such a great girl to sit at home waiting till her relative came to Athens from all that way off? That was what you should have urged, father, and pleaded.

MICIO: Absurd! Was I to plead against the interest of the man whom I had come to help as a witness? But what have we to do with this, Aeschinus, or what are these women to us? Let us be going. [*As Aeschinus breaks down and weeps*] What's the matter? Why are you in tears?

AESCHINUS: I beseech you, father, listen to me.

MICIO: I have heard all, Aeschinus, and I know all; I love you, and so I take all the more interest in your doings.

AESCHINUS: As I hope, father, that I shall deserve your love as long as I live, so I declare that I am deeply grieved at having committed this fault, and I am ashamed of myself in your sight.

MICIO: I verily believe you, for I know your honourable character; but I fear you are too remiss in this matter. In what city do you suppose that you are living? Here you have seduced a young lady whom you had no right to touch. This was your first sin, and a great one; a great sin, but after all, human nature. Many good men have done the same. But after that, pray did you ever think the matter over, or look forward on your own account to what would have to be done? If you were ashamed to tell me this story yourself how was I to learn it? While you were hesitating, ten months have slipped away. You have, as far as in you lay, betrayed yourself and this poor girl and the child. What! Did you suppose that the gods would manage this business for you while you lay asleep, and that she would be brought home to you and installed in your bedroom without your taking any trouble about it? I hope you won't manage other business so negligently. Now be of good cheer, she shall be your wife.

AESCHINUS: What?

MICIO: Be of good cheer, I say.

AESCHINUS: Father, I beseech you, are you mocking me?

MICIO: Mocking you? Why should I?

AESCHINUS: I don't know; but I am so terribly anxious that this should be true, that I am all the more inclined to doubt it.

MICIO: Go home, and pray to the gods that you may bring home your bride; off with you!

AESCHINUS: What? My bride already?

MICIO: Already.

AESCHINUS: What? Now?

MICIO: As soon as may be.

AESCHINUS: Father, may all the gods abhor me if I don't love you better than my own eyes.

MICIO: What? Better than her?

AESCHINUS: Just as much.

MICIO: [*Smiling*] That's very kind of you.

AESCHINUS: I say, where's that man from Miletus?

MICIO: He's gone; he's gone on board ship. But why do you linger here?

AESCHINUS: Father, you go and pray to the gods, rather than I, for I am quite sure that they will be more likely to hear your prayers, as you are a far better man than I.

MICIO: I'll go into the house to make what preparations are necessary; you, if you are wise, do as I have said. [*Micio goes inside*]

AESCHINUS: [*To himself*] What's this? Is this to be a father or to be a son? What more could he do for me if he were my brother or my bosom friend? Is he not a man to be loved? To be carried next one's heart? His kindness, however, has made me very anxious; for fear that through carelessness I may do something that will displease him. I must be on my guard. But why don't I go into the house, that I may not myself delay my own marriage?

[*Aeschinus goes inside*]

---

## SCENE VI

*[Enter Demea wearily]*

DEMEA: *[To himself]* I have walked till I'm dead tired. Syrus, may great Jove confound you with your directions. I have crawled about all over the town-to the gate, to the pond; where haven't I been? There was no carpenter's shop there, and not a soul said he had seen my brother. Now I've made up my mind to wait for him in his house till he returns.

## SCENE VII

*[Enter Micio from his house]*

MICIO: *[To Aeschinus within]* I'll go and tell them that there shall be no delay on our part.

DEMEA: Why, there's the man himself. I have long been seeking you, Micio.

MICIO: What for?

DEMEA: I bring you news of more outrageous wickedness done by that nice young man.

MICIO: More, eh?

DEMEA: Hanging matters.

MICIO: Oh, nonsense.

DEMEA: You don't know what sort of a man he is.

MICIO: Yes, I do.

DEMEA: Fool, you are mooning, thinking that I mean the affair of the music girl; but this is a rape committed on a young lady, a citizen of Athens.

MICIO: Yes, I know.

DEMEA: What? You know of it and you endure it?

MICIO: Why shouldn't I endure it?

DEMEA: Tell me, don't you cry out at it? Doesn't it drive you mad?

MICIO: No, it does not. I might have preferred-

DEMEA: There is a baby boy born.

MICIO: Heaven bless him!

DEMEA: The girl hasn't a penny.

MICIO: So I have heard.

DEMEA: And she is to be married without a dowry.

MICIO: Of course.

DEMEA: What's to be done now?

MICIO: What the occasion requires; the girl must be brought over from that house to this.

DEMEA: O Jupiter! Is that the way that you ought to take it?

MICIO: What more can I do?

DEMEA: What can you do? Why, if you are not really put out at this, at any rate it would be your duty to pretend that you are.

MICIO: Why, I have betrothed the girl to him; the whole affair is settled; the wedding is just going to take place. I have set them free from all fear; this was much more my duty.

DEMEA: But, Micio, do you approve of what he has done?

MICIO: No, not if I could alter it; but since I can't, I make the best of it. The life of man is like playing with dice: if you don't throw exactly what you want, you must use your wits to make shift with what you have thrown.

DEMEA: Make shift, indeed! By this use of your wits you have lost twenty minae for that music girl, whom you must now dispose of for nothing, if you can't sell her.

MICIO: I shall not; nor do I want to sell her.

DEMEA: Then what will you do with her?

MICIO: She will live with us.

DEMEA: Heavens and earth! A mistress and a wife in the same household?

MICIO: Why not?

DEMEA: Do you think you're in your right mind?

MICIO: I believe so.

DEMEA: So help me heaven, when I consider what a fool you are, I believe that you mean to keep her to give you music lessons!

MICIO:  Why shouldn't she?

DEMEA: And will she give the bride music lessons too?

MICIO: Of course she will.

DEMEA: And you will dance "the ladies' chain" between them, I suppose?

MICIO: Very well.

DEMEA: Very well?

MICIO: Yes; and you shall join us, if need be.

DEMEA: Damn it! Aren't you ashamed of this?

MICIO:  Now, Demea, just put away this ill temper of yours, and be merry and good humoured, as you ought to be, on your son's wedding-day. I'll go and see the ladies, and then I'll come back here again. [Micio goes into Sostrata's house]

DEMEA: [*To himself*] Oh, Jupiter, what a life! What morals! What folly! A bride without a dowry is to be brought home; there's a music girl in the house; an extravagant establishment; a youth given over to debauchery, an old dotard. Why, the goddess of Salvation could not save this household, even if she wanted to.

# ACT V

## SCENE I

*[Enter Syrus from the house]*

SYRUS: *[Drunk, talking to himself]* Faith, Syry, my boy, you've done finely for yourself and managed your part of the business sumptuously. Well, now that I've had a bellyful of all sorts of good things indoors, I've taken a fancy to a stroll out in front of the house here.

DEMEA: See, there's an instance of the way the household is kept in order.

SYRUS: Why, here's our old gentleman. How goes it? What are you so gloomy about?

DEMEA: Oh, you scoundrel!

SYRUS: Shut up! None of your jaw here, old wise-acre!

DEMEA: If you were my slave--

SYRUS: You'd have been a rich man, Demea, and have made your fortune.

DEMEA: I'd see that you were made a warning to all men.

SYRUS: What for? What harm have I done?

DEMEA: Do you ask me? Why, just at the very crisis, and after the worst of wrongdoing, you get drunk, you scoundrel, before things have even been quieted down, just as if you had done some good action.

SYRUS: [*Aside*] Oh, hell! I wish I'd stayed indoors.


## SCENE II

[*Dromo appears in the doorway*]

DROMO: Here, Syrus, Ctesipho wants you to come back.

SYRUS: Get along with you!

[*Dromo disappears*]

DEMEA: Ctesipho here! What's that he says?

SYRUS: Nothing.

DEMEA: Is Ctesipho here, scoundrel?

SYRUS: No.

DEMEA: Then why did he mention his name?

SYRUS: It's another man, a little parasite chap. Don't you know him?

DEMEA: I will directly. [He approaches the door]

SYRUS: What are you doing? Where are you going to? [*Catching hold of Demea*]

DEMEA: Let me go! [*Threatens him*]

SYRUS: I say, don't.

DEMEA: Will you take your hands off me, you villain, or do you prefer to have your brains knocked out here? [*Demea dashes into the house*]

SYRUS: He's gone. A damned unwelcome addition to their wine party, especially to Ctesipho. What am I to do now?
Better get out of the way somewhere into a corner, and sleep off this drop of wine, until all these rows quiet down; that's what I'll do. [*Syrus goes inside unsteadily*]


## SCENE III

[*Enter Micio from Sostrata's house*]

MICIO: [*To Sostrata within*] We have everything ready, as I told you, Sostrata; so when you like-Why, who is that knocking so loud at my door?

[*Re-enter Demea from Micio's house*]

DEMEA: [*To himself*] Oh, dear me! What shall I do? What's to be done? How can I cry aloud and lament enough? O heavens, earth, and seas!

MICIO: [*Aside*] There you are! He has found out the whole story; you may be sure that that's what he's crying out about. There'll be a row. I must try to help.

DEMEA: See, there he is, the debaucher of both our sons!

MICIO: Pray restrain your passion and calm yourself.

DEMEA: I have restrained it. I am calm. I don't say another word of abuse. Let us look at the facts. Was it not arranged between us (you started the arrangement) that you were not to meddle with my son, and I was not to meddle with yours? Answer me.

MICIO: It was; I don't deny it.

DEMEA: Then why is he now drinking in your house? Why do you harbour my boy, Micio? Why do you buy a mistress for him? Isn't it fair that I should have as much rights over my son as you have over yours? Since I don't look after your son, don't you look after mine.

MICIO: What you say is not fair; no, it isn't; for it is an old proverb that friends have all things in common.

DEMEA: How clever! But this suggestion is a little late, isn't it?

MICIO: If you don't mind, Demea, listen while I say a few words. First of all, if you are vexed at the extravagance of your sons, pray bear these facts in mind. You, in the beginning, were going to bring up both your sons as your means permitted, because you supposed that your fortune would be enough for both of them, and of course you thought at that time that I should marry. Well, you keep on in that same old style now: pinch, scrape, and be stingy. Take care to leave them as large a fortune as ever you can, and glory in doing so. But let them use my fortune, which is available for them contrary to their expectations. Your property will not suffer thereby. What you get from me you may count as clear gain. If you would think these things over impartially, Demea, you would save both me and yourself and the boys much unpleasantness.

DEMEA: I pass over the expense; but their morals--

MICIO: Stay. I know; I was coming to that. There are many signs in people's characters whereby you may easily guess, when two of them are doing the same thing, how it will affect them, so that you can often say: "It will do this one no harm, it will do that one harm"; not because the thing that they are doing is different, but because their characters are different. Now by what I see of them, I am confident that they will turn out as we wish, I see that they are sensible, intelligent, high-minded, and fond of one another. You can see that they are gentlemen in thought and disposition; you can pull them in any day you please. Perhaps you are afraid that they are rather neglectful of business. Oh, my dear Demea, as we grow older we grow wiser about everything else, but the one vice which age brings to us, is that of being keener after money-making than we ought to be. Time will make them sharp enough at that.

DEMEA: Always provided, Micio, that your specious reasoning and easy good nature does not do them too much harm.

MICIO: Hush, I shall not do that. Now let us say no more about this business; be my guest today and clear your brow.

DEMEA: Well, it seems to be the fashion; I must do so; but at break of day I am off to the country with my son.

MICIO: Oh, tonight, for all I care; only do be cheerful today.

DEMEA: And I'll take that music girl away with me.

MICIO: Then you will have won your battle. By so doing you will quite gain your son's heart; only mind you keep her.

DEMEA: I will see to that: at the farm I'll make her cook and grind corn till she's all over ashes and smoke and flour; besides, I'll make her go gleaning under the noonday sun; I'll burn her as black as a coal.

MICIO: Right; now you seem to me to be showing good sense; and there I'd make him sleep with her, even if he doesn't want to.

DEMEA: Are you laughing at me? Well, you are lucky to be able to take it so. I feel

MICIO: Now, no more of that.

DEMEA: Well, I'm just leaving off.

MICIO: Then come into the house, and let us spend this day as we ought. [*They go into Micio's house. A short time is supposed to elapse before the next scene.*]


## SCENE IV

[*Enter Demea from Micio's house*]

DEMEA: [*To himself*] No man ever lived in so well-regulated a fashion but what circumstances, years, and experience must continually present something new to him, and suggest something to him; so that you don't know what you once thought you knew, and cast away what you once supposed to be of the first importance. That is what's happened to me, for now, when my time is almost spent, I renounce the severe life that I have hitherto lived. Why do I do that? Because I have been taught by circumstances that nothing suits a man better than easygoing good nature. Anybody could tell this easily by comparing me and my brother. He has always spent his life at leisure, and in entertainments, in good humour, with unruffled temper, giving no man a harsh word, with a smile for everyone: he has lived to please himself, and has spent money on himself alone; well, all men speak well of him and love him. I, the countryman, rude, harsh, stingy, ill-tempered and self-willed, I married, and what wretchedness I went through. Sons were born: more trouble; and then, why, dear me! in trying to do the best I can for them, I have wasted all my life and manhood. Now, at the end of my days, what is my reward at their hands? Dislike; while that brother of mine has all a father's pleasures without the trouble. They are fond of him, and they run away from me. They tell him all their secrets, they love him, they are both at his house, and I am left alone. They hope that he will live, while of course they look forward to my death. Thus, for a small outlay, he has made them into his own sons, after I had brought them up with enormous trouble. I get all the pain, and he enjoys all the pleasure. Come, come now, let us try the other tack; let me see whether I can speak gently or behave kindly, since my brother challenges me to do so. I also demand to be loved and thought much of by my people; if that can be got by giving them presents and humouring their whim, I will not be behindhand. There will be a deficit in my exchequer, but that won't matter to me, seeing that I am the elder brother.

## SCENE V

*[Enter Syrus from Micio's house]*

SYRUS: Demea, your brother begs you to keep near the house.

DEMEA: Who's there? Oh, my good Syrus! How goes it? How's all with you?

SYRUS: Very well.

DEMEA: [*Aside*] I'm getting on capitally. There, for the first time in my life I have forced myself, against my true character, to add these three sayings, "My good," "how goes it?" and "how's all with you?" [*Aloud*] You are not a badly behaved slave, and I should be glad to do you some service.

SYRUS: Much obliged.

DEMEA: Indeed, Syrus, this is true, and facts will prove it to you before long.

## SCENE VI

[*Enter Geta from Sostrata's house*]

GETA: [*To Sostrata within*] I'm going across to our neighbours', ma'am, to see when they will be ready to fetch the young lady. [*Looking round*] Why, there is Demea! Good day, sir.

DEMEA: Oh, what's your name?

GETA: Geta.

DEMEA: Geta, I have today made up my mind that you are an invaluable fellow, for I think that the worth of a slave is thoroughly proved when he is zealous for his owner, as I have noticed you are, Geta, and for that I shall be pleased to be of service to you whenever I have an opportunity. [Aside] I am studying how to be amiable, and really making progress.

GETA: You are very good to think so.

DEMEA: [*Aside*] I am beginning with the mob and gradually winning their affections.

# SCENE VII

*[Enter Aeschinus from Micio's house]*

AESCHINUS: *[To himself]* They plague me to death, wanting to make such an ultra-solemn wedding of it; they are wasting the whole day with their preparations.

DEMEA: How goes it, Aeschinus?

AESCHINUS: Why, father, are you here?

DEMEA: Yes, your father both in will and in deed, who loves you more than his own eyes. Why don't you bring home your bride?

AESCHINUS: I want to, but I am waiting for flute-players and people to sing the wedding hymn.

DEMEA: Now, will you take the advice of an old man like me?

AESCHINUS: What do you advise?

DEMEA: Get rid of the wedding procession, hymns, torches, flute-players and all, and order this party-wall in the garden to be pulled down as soon as may be. Bring your bride through that way; throw the two houses into one. Bring her mother and all her house-hold over to us.

AESCHINUS: Well said, my most charming father.

DEMEA: *[Aside]* Capital! I'm called charming already. My brother's house will become a thoroughfare; he will take a host of people into it, he will spend much money in entertaining them, there will be lots of expenses-well! what do I care? I am charming, and making myself popular. [*To Aeschinus*] Here, order old Croesus to pay you twenty minae straightway. Syrus, why don't you go and do what you are ordered?

SYRUS: What am I to do?

DEMEA: Pull down the wall. [*To Geta, as Syrus goes inside*] You go and bring the ladies through the garden.

GETA: May the gods bless you, Demea, for I see that you are a true well-wisher to our family.
DEMEA: I think that they deserve it. [*To Aeschinus, as Geta goes into Sostrata's house*] What do you say?

AESCHINUS: I quite agree.

DEMEA: It is much more proper than that she should be brought here along the public road, being ill and weak after childbirth.

AESCHINUS: Father, I never saw anything better arranged.

DEMEA: That's the way I always do arrange things; but see, here's Micio coming out of his house.

## SCENE VIII

[*Enter Micio, somewhat upset*]

MICIO: [To the men within who are pulling down the wall] My brother's orders, d'ye say? Where is my brother? [Seeing him] Are these your orders, Demea?

DEMEA: My orders are both in this and all other matters to make one household of it as far as may be, to cherish, help, and unite them.

AESCHINUS: Do so, father, I pray you.

MICIO: I think that we ought.

DEMEA: Nay, it's our duty so to do. In the first place, this bride has a mother.

MICIO: She has; what then?

DEMEA: An honest and discreet lady.

MICIO: So they say.

DEMEA: She's a trifle elderly.

MICIO: I know that she is.

DEMEA: She has long been too old to bear children, and she has no one to take care of her, a lone woman.

MICIO: [*Aside*] What is he driving at?

DEMEA: [*To Micio*] It is your duty to marry her, and [*to Aeschinus*] yours to see that he does so.

MICIO: Me marry!

DEMEA: Yes, you.

MICIO: Me?

DEMEA: Yes, you, I say.

MICIO: Nonsense.

DEMEA: [*To Aeschinus*] If you're a man, he'll do it.

AESCHINUS: Father, dear.

MICIO: What, you young donkey, are you giving ear to his proposals?

DEMEA: It is no use, you cannot help doing it

MICIO You're out of your mind.

AESCHINUS: Let me win your consent, father.

MICIO: You're mad; be off with you.

DEMEA: Come, do your son this favour.

MICIO: Are you in your right senses? Am I, in my sixty-fifth year, to become a bridegroom for the first time, and marry a decrepit old woman? Is that what-you seriously propose that I should do?

AESCHINUS: Do it, father; I have promised them that you will.

MICIO: Promised, have you! Promise what is your own to give, my boy.

DEMEA: Come! Suppose he were to ask some greater favour of you.

MICIO: As if this wasn't the greatest of all!

DEMEA: Grant it.

AESCHINUS: Don't be cross.

DEMEA: Do it; promise you will do it.

MICIO Leave me alone, can't you?

DEMEA: I won't, till you give your consent.

MICIO: This is assault and battery.

DEMEA: Behave generously, Micio.

MICIO: Although this marriage seems to me to be a mistaken, absurd, foolish proceeding, yet if you are so eager for it, let it take place.

AESCHINUS: You are right.

DEMEA: You deserve my affection; but--

MICIO: But what?

DEMEA: Now that I have got my wish, I will tell you.

MICIO: What next? What more am I to do?

DEMEA: The next of kin to these ladies, who is now a connection of ours is Hegio, a poor man; it is our duty to do something for him.

MICIO: What are we to do?

DEMEA: There is a small piece of land here just outside the city, which you let out on hire. Let us give him the use of it.

MICIO: A small piece, d'ye call it?

DEMEA: If it were a big one, still you ought to do it; he has been like a father to her, he is a good man, and one of ourselves now; it is right to give it to him. Besides, I am now myself putting into practice the maxim which you, Micio, enunciated so wisely and so well a short time ago: "A vice common to all mankind is that of being too keen after money when we are old." It is our duty to put away this reproach from us; your maxim is a true one, and should be acted upon.

AESCHINUS: Dear father.

MICIO: Well, well, he shall have it, since Aeschinus so wishes it.

AESCHINUS: I am delighted.

DEMEA: Now you are truly my brother alike in body and in soul. [*Aside*] I am cutting his throat with his own sword.

## SCENE IX

[*Enter Syrus*]

SYRUS: I have done what you ordered, Demea.

DEMEA: You're an honest fellow; and now my opinion is that this day Syrus ought to be made a free man.

MICIO: Him a free man? Why, what for?

DEMEA: For many things.

SYRUS: Oh, dear Demea, you are indeed a good man. I have watched over both your sons for you ever since they were boys with the greatest care; I have taught them and admonished them, and always given them the best advice that I could.

DEMEA: The facts prove that you did; moreover, you can be trusted to buy fish for dinner, you can bring a courtesan into the house, and you can prepare a feast in the middle of the day. It requires no ordinary man to do this.

SYRUS: What a pleasant old gentleman!

DEMEA: Moreover, he helped today to buy the music girl. He managed the business, and he ought to be repaid for his trouble.
The other slaves will be all the better for the example; besides, Aeschinus wishes it.

MICIO: [*To Aeschinus*] Do you wish it?

AESCHINUS: I do.

MICIO: Well, if you wish it: [*To Syrus*] Syrus, come here to me. [*Strikes him with a stick*] Be a free man.

SYRUS: 'Tis generously done: I return my thanks to you all; and to you in particular, Demea.

DEMEA: I rejoice at it.

AESCHINUS: And I too.

SYRUS: I believe it. I wish this my joy were complete, and that I might see my wife Phrygia free too.

DEMEA: An excellent woman, truly!

SYRUS: And the first that suckled my young master's son, your grandson today.

DEMEA: Indeed? Why, if she really was the first that suckled him, without any question she ought to be made free.

MICIO: What, for that?
DEMEA: For that: in fine, you shall have the price of her freedom from me.

SYRUS: May the gods ever grant you all your desires, Demea!

MICIO: Syrus, you've done nicely for yourself today.

DEMEA: Moreover, brother, if you'll do your duty and let him have a little ready money to begin with he'll soon repay it.

MICIO: Not this much. [*Snapping his fingers*]

AESCHINUS: He's an industrious honest fellow.

SYRUS: I'll return it, indeed; only let me have it.

AESCHINUS: Do, father.

MICIO: I'll consider it.

DEMEA: He'll do it.

SYRUS: O excellent man!

AESCHINUS: O delightful father!

MICIO: What means all this, brother? Whence this sudden change in your temper? What is this whim? What a hasty fit of prodigality!

DEMEA: I'll tell you, in order to make you realize that your passing for an easy agreeable man is not genuine, or founded on equity and good sense, but due to your overlooking things, your indulgence, and giving them whatever they want. Now, Aeschinus, I am, therefore, odious to you, because I don't wholly humour you in everything right or wrong. I'll concern myself with you no farther; squander buy, do whatever you have a mind to. But if you
had rather that I check and restrain you in pursuit which, by reason of your youth, - you are not aware of the consequences of, when passion misleads you or prompts you too far, and that I direct you, as occasion offers: behold me ready to do you that service.

AESCHINUS: Father, we submit to you entirely: you best know what is fit and proper. But how will you do with my brother?

DEMEA: I consent that he may have his girl, provided his follies end there.

AESCHINUS: That's well. [*To the spectators*] Give us your applause.

**TERENCE** (Publius Terentius Afer) was born in Africa, and in his youth was brought to Rome as a slave. The name of his family is unknown, but when he was set free he took that of Terentius, from his master Terentius Lucanus. He began to write in the year 166 B.C., and continued with increasing success till his death.

Owing to the loss of Menander's plays, the later, or new comedy of the Greeks is known to us only by the plays of Plautus and Terence; and superior as Plautus was in brightness and originality, the dignity of Terence's style, and the purity of his Latin, so strange in an African slave, have made him for the moderns the chief representative of the ancient comedy of private life. Hence his enormous influence in literature; for Cervantes, Shakespeare, and Moliere have all been indebted to him. Such plays as Les Fourberies de Scapin breathe the very spirit of the ancient comedy.

Terence took the plots of his six plays from the Greek, and much of his work is merely translation, so that it is difficult to tell how far its merits are his own or Menander's; but one of his most successful characters, the insolent parasite, Phormio, who is yet ever ready, faithful, and undaunted in the service of his friends, comes in a play taken from a very inferior dramatist. His plots and characters are drawn from a narrow and somewhat conventional field. The troubles of young men in love, and their efforts to outwit their elders, with the aid of clever slaves and parasites, form the general groundwork; and a favourite way out of the difficulties is the discovery that the girl in question has been lost or stolen in childhood, and is really of a most respectable family. The slaves of Terence are a wonderful study to those who reflect on the story of his life. They are always on the side of youth and pleasure, full of impudence and resource, -often with a fidelity to their chosen part, unshaken even by the sound of the whip and the chains which we hear behind all. The comedy of the ancients did not allow of characters showing the extremes of heroism or baseness, but in Terence all are marked by some redeeming qualities.

The suspicious fathers and dissolute sons, crafty slaves and overbearing masters, braggarts, parasites, and courtesans have all some share of kindly human feeling and good fellowship. The words of Terence so often quoted may stand as the very essence of his moral teaching: "Homo sum, humani nihil a me alienum puto" I am man; and think there is nothing human but claims my sympathies.

*This biography is reprinted from The New Calendar of Great Men. Ed. Frederic Harrison. London: Macmillan and Co., 1920.*

# About The Author

Charles David Brooks, III is Assistant Professor of Theater and the Director of the Theatre Ensemble at Benedict College. His studies include a Master's in Fine Arts (Directing) from the University of California at Los Angeles, and a Master's in Educational Administration from Teachers College, Columbia University, New York. He's done extensive field research study, which allowed him to eloquently pen this book of plays.

In 2007, Professor Brooks journeyed to Egypt, and in 2009, to Ethiopia with the Kemet Nu "Know Thyself" Educational Tours, a part of the African-Centered Lectures sponsored by Ashra and Merira Kwesi, lecturers on African history, civilization, religion, and culture. In 2010, he participated in the Benedict College Office of International Programs Summer Research Fellow / Fundación Curduvaré that took him to Venezuela. He also conducted field research in 2011 on his Sankofa Journey to Ghana to study the Ashanti history and religion.

He is a member of the Actors' Equity, an American labor union representing the world of live theater. As an actor, he has performed in movies, television, and on stage. As a card-carrying member of the Stage Directors and Choreographers Society, he has directed in theaters from the renowned Lincoln Center in New York to stages in Los Angeles, California.

Made in the USA
Columbia, SC
07 May 2024

35040072R00113